Better Homes and Gardens.

STEP-BY-STEP
CABINETS
& SHELVES

BETTER HOMES AND GARDENS® BOOKS
Editor: Gerald M. Knox
Art Director: Ernest Shelton
Managing Editor: David A. Kirchner

Building and Remodeling Editor: Joan McCloskey
Building Books Editor: Larry Clayton
Building Books Associate Editor: Jim Harrold

Associate Art Director (Managing): Randall Yontz
Associate Art Directors (Creative): Linda Ford,
    Neoma Alt West
Copy and Production Editors: Marsha Jahns,
    Nancy Nowiszewski, Mary Helen Schiltz,
    David A. Walsh
Assistant Art Directors: Harijs Priekulis, Tom Wegner
Graphic Designers: Mike Burns, Alisann Dixon,
    Mike Eagleton, Lynda Haupert, Deb Miner,
    Lyne Neymeyer, Trish Church-Podlasek, Stan Sams,
    D. Greg Thompson, Darla Whipple, Paul Zimmerman

Editor in Chief: Neil Kuehnl
Group Editorial Services Director: Duane Gregg

General Manager: Fred Stines
Director of Publishing: Robert B. Nelson
Director of Retail Marketing: Jamie Martin
Director of Direct Marketing: Arthur Heydendael

Step-By-Step Cabinets and Shelves
Editors: Larry Clayton, Jim Harrold
Copy and Production Editor: Mary Helen Schiltz
Graphic Designer: Mike Burns
Technical Consultants: Jim Downing,
    George Granseth, Don Wipperman
Drawings: Carson Ode

CONTENTS

Introduction   4

Tools of the Trade   6

Materials and Hardware   8

Lumber, 9 . . . Moldings, 11 . . . Sheet Goods, 12 . . . Counter-Top Materials, 14 . . . Finishing Materials, 16 . . . Manufactured Cabinet and Shelving Components, 17 . . . Hardware (Fasteners, Glues and Adhesives, Shelf Supports, Cabinet Hardware), 18

Planning Guidelines   22

First Things First, 23 . . . Know Your Construction Options, 24 . . . Typical Dimensions, 32 . . . Commit Your Plan to Paper, 34

The ABC's of Cabinet Construction   36

Assembling the Cabinet Shell, 37 . . . Attaching the Face Frame, 40 . . . Adding Shelves, 41 . . . Adding Doors, 44 . . . Adding Drawers, 50 . . . Applying a Finish to the Cabinet, 52 . . . Installing Cabinets, 54 . . . Installing Counter Tops (Site-Built and Manufactured), 55 . . . Surfacing Counter Tops with Ceramic Tile, 60

Cutting and Joining Techniques   62

Making Basic Cuts (with a Portable Circular Saw, Table Saw, Router), 63 . . . Joining Cabinet Members (Joinery Types, Joining with Nails, Screws, or Dowels and Glue), 75

Project Potpourri   78

Glossary   94

Index   95

INTRODUCTION

Most people assume that being able to fashion good-looking shelving and cabinetry projects is the exclusive domain of the professional cabinetmaker. But that's simply not the case. Sure, a professional has the advantage of many years of experience and a thorough knowledge of his trade—both big pluses.

But if you're willing to invest some time and effort in learning the art of cabinetmaking, we're sure you can achieve results that will please you and anyone else who views your handiwork. Not only that, but we'll also guarantee you that you'll get a lot of satisfaction from a job well done—and save

a considerable amount of money by building your own units rather than purchasing manufactured ones or hiring out the work.

It would take a book many times larger than this one to explain all of the nuances of the cabinetmaker's trade. But that's not our goal—just as it's probably not yours to learn them all.

In this book we concentrate on the basics—those things you need to know to achieve good results, whether you're taking on an easy-to-construct shelving unit or a more demanding project such as a bank of

kitchen cabinets. Every effort has been made not to overwhelm you with optional information.

The book opens with a survey of the tools of the cabinetmaker's trade on pages 6 and 7. You may already have many of the tools you'll need.

Then we turn immediately to the first major section, "Materials and Hardware." Basically an awareness and buymanship chapter, this is where you'll learn about choosing and buying the various items needed to build your projects. Included is information on millwork lumber, moldings, and sheet goods as well as counter-top and finishing materials, manufactured cabinet and shelving components, and last but not least, hardware.

Once you know what's what in materials and hardware, you can then set about developing your project plan. On pages 22-35, in the "Planning Guidelines" section, we walk you through the entire planning process. We help you decide what size, shape, and style of unit is best for you, show you your various construction options and the typical dimensions for several types of projects, and teach you how to draw your plan on graph paper, as well as make materials lists and cutting diagrams.

After you've charted your course by developing a plan, you're ready for section 3, "The ABC's of Cabinet Construction." Here, we take you step by step through the cabinet-building process, starting with assembling the cabinet shell, then on to adding the face frame, adding shelves, building and installing doors and drawers, applying a paint or clear finish, installing the cabinet itself, installing counter tops, and working with plastic laminate and ceramic tile.

In the book's fourth major section, "Cutting and Joining Techniques," you'll learn how to make a variety of basic cuts with circular and table saws and a router. In addition, we explain several ways to join cabinet and shelving members together, as well as the role clamping plays in quality construction.

On page 78, we begin the final chapter, "Project Potpourri." This 16-page segment features eight inspiring projects that you can build as described or alter to suit your needs. We've included a cutaway drawing and full step-by-step instructions with each.

Tools of the Trade

Doing any job well requires that you use the right tools. This holds particularly true when building cabinets and shelving units, where there is no room for shoddy workmanship. At right are the basic tools needed to construct any project contained in the book. Later, in the chapter entitled "Cutting and Joining Techniques," we'll explain how to use the more sophisticated tools, such as certain power tools and the doweling jig.

Remember, though, that when using tools, safety comes first. Before operating the power tools shown here, see the safety pointers on page 62.

1 Because accurate measuring stands behind every well-crafted project, purchase a quality **flexible steel tape**. A 12-footer with a lock-button should suffice for most measuring tasks.

2 Keep corners perpendicular with a **framing square**.

3 A **level** can tell you that the project you're attaching to the wall is horizontal and/or vertical. Buy a handy two-foot model.

4 Mark cutoff lines and make pilot holes with an **awl**.

5 Let a **straightedge** help you strike cut lines or guide such power tools as the circular saw or router.

6 A **T-bevel** specializes in duplicating angles.

7 Snap long, straight lines with a **chalk reel**.

8 Use a **block plane** to shave the end grain of wood.

9 To do mortise work, to clean out dadoes and grooves, or for general shaping and refining, pick up a set of metal-capped **chisels**.

10 Touch up rough edges and other trouble spots with a **wood file**. The best purchase here is a coarse, half-round, double-cut file.

11 Keep a **rasp** handy, too, to grate off irregularities too time-consuming to do with a wood file.

12 Let a 26-inch, 8-point crosscut **handsaw** perform any general-purpose cutting.

13 For intricate cutting around curves, no other hand-held saw can compete with the **coping saw**.

14 Drive finish nails into cabinet and shelving members using a lightweight 10- or 13-ounce **hammer**.

15 Then recess the heads of the finish nails with a **nail set**.

16, 17 Drive screws with **slotted** or **Phillips-tipped screwdrivers**.

18 Spread filler over nail holes and other voids using a **putty knife**.

19, 20, 21, 22, 23 To assist in gluing and joining materials, purchase **miter clamps** to secure corners, **C-clamps** or **hand screws** for joining materials face to face, **pipe clamps** for spanning long distances, and **strap clamps** for joining large or odd-shaped constructions.

24, 25 To join members using dowels, you'll need a precision **dowel jig** and **doweling bit**.

26 Wear **safety glasses** when operating power tools.

27, 28, 29 Rabbet, dado, or do fancy edge work with a **router**. When buying one, also pick up a variety of **bits** and an **edge guide**.

30 Keep a **belt sander** on hand to quickly smooth uneven joints or any other rough spots.

31, 32 Cut cabinet and shelving pieces to size, or fashion dadoes or rabbets using a **portable circular saw**. Convert this tool into a table saw by mounting it to a **circular saw table attachment**.

33 Or, ensure accuracy and speed by investing in a **table saw**—the woodworker's premier cutting tool.

34 Along with the saw, purchase a **plywood blade**, a **combination blade** for general ripping and crosscutting, and a **hollow ground blade** for fine cutting. Or, if you want just one blade to make all of the above cuts, purchase a more expensive **40-tooth carbide-tipped blade**.

35 And to cut out circles or other shapes, complete your tool collection by adding a **saber saw** and **fine, medium,** and **coarse blades**.

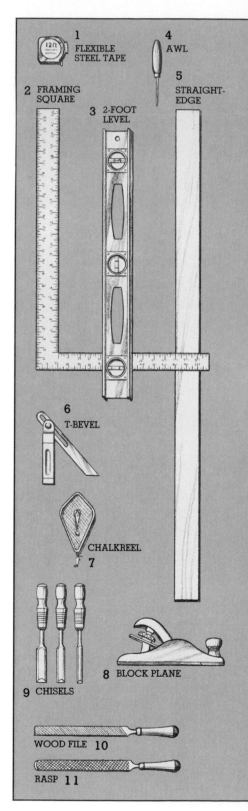

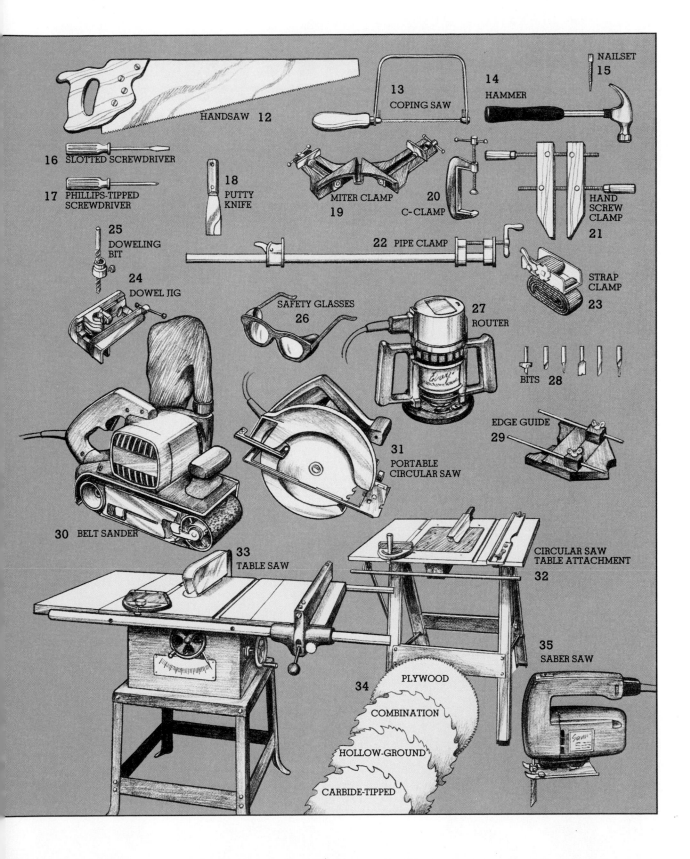

HANDSAW 12
13 COPING SAW
14 HAMMER
NAILSET 15
16 SLOTTED SCREWDRIVER
17 PHILLIPS-TIPPED SCREWDRIVER
18 PUTTY KNIFE
MITER CLAMP 19
20 C-CLAMP
HAND SCREW CLAMP 21
25 DOWELING BIT
24 DOWEL JIG
22 PIPE CLAMP
STRAP CLAMP 23
SAFETY GLASSES 26
27 ROUTER
BITS 28
EDGE GUIDE 29
31 PORTABLE CIRCULAR SAW
30 BELT SANDER
33 TABLE SAW
CIRCULAR SAW TABLE ATTACHMENT 32
35 SABER SAW
34 PLYWOOD
COMBINATION
HOLLOW-GROUND
CARBIDE-TIPPED

MATERIALS AND HARDWARE

In the chapter entitled "Planning Guidelines," we point out the necessity of having a plan to work from when building a shelving or cabinetry project. And that's good advice. But there's something that precedes even the plan—and is equally as important—acquainting yourself with the materials and hardware available to you as a cabinetmaker.

As you do this, you will begin to see the possibilities that lie before you in terms of flexibility of design and construction. You will also gain an appreciation of how extensive your material and hardware options are.

We begin this chapter with a discussion of how to choose and buy millwork lumber, the type you'll be using for your projects. Particularly useful are the three charts that deal with the species, sizes, and grades of millwork lumber commonly available. As you'll see, knowing how to order this material requires some savvy on your part.

Next, we introduce you to the various types of moldings you will come in contact with when you visit a building materials dealer. You'll also learn how to estimate your needs as well as how to save money when purchasing moldings.

Then, because sheet goods figure so prominently in most projects, we supply a chart listing your alternatives—with special emphasis on plywood—as well as pointers on purchasing these items.

And to round out the chapter, we include sections on counter-top and finishing materials, manufactured cabinet and shelving components, and hardware.

Choosing and Buying Millwork Lumber

If you've never purchased millwork lumber for a shelving unit or cabinet, you might assume that ordering it must be similar to the way you'd order dimension lumber. Not so! On this and the following page we give you a rundown on what you need to know before you step up to the service counter and place your order.

What Is Millwork Lumber?

Though millwork is technically "woodwork that has been machined at a planing mill," for the purpose of this book, millwork lumber is any top-quality lumber (including molding) used in the building of shelving units, cabinets, and fine furniture. As you can see in the species chart on page 10, most millwork lumber comes from hardwood timber; pine is the only commonly used softwood represented. The chart tells a bit about the more popular species. Which one you use for a project is a matter of personal preference.

For more information about a particular species, visit a local millwork dealer. Personnel there are generally quite knowledgeable as well as helpful.

Very few building materials dealers stock more than a few millwork selections. To locate one who specializes in millwork items, refer to the Yellow Pages of your phone book, under Millwork or Lumber.

How Is It Sized and Graded?

Unlike dimension lumber, which manufacturers mill to industry-established thicknesses, widths, and lengths, most millwork lumber comes in random lengths and widths. And there's a reason for this. Because of the relative scarcity of these woods, it is cost prohibitive to mill each piece to a certain size and dispose of the scrap material that would result.

As with dimension lumber, huge differences in quality exist in millwork lumber. Recognizing this, the National Hardwood Lumber Association has developed a hardwood grading system. The Western Wood Products Association has done the same for pine lumber. The chart on page 10 lists the various grades and describes characteristics that wood in a certain grade has.

Placing Your Order

When you go to purchase your lumber, you'll find assorted boards of various thicknesses in stacks or bins *(continued)*

Common Millwork Lumber Sizes			
Thickness	**Actual**	**Pine**	**Uses**
⅝" material	(½" or ⁷⁄₁₆")	(same)	Drawer sides and backs
1" material	(²⁵⁄₃₂")	(same)	Cabinet facings, base frames, shelving, cabinet ledgers
1¼" material	(1¹⁄₁₆")	(1⁵⁄₃₂")	Shelving, shelf supports, furniture parts
1½" material	(1⁵⁄₁₆")	(1¹³⁄₃₂")	Shelving, shelf supports, furniture parts
2" material	(1¾")	(1¹³⁄₁₆")	Shelving supports, furniture parts, mantels

Choosing and Buying Millwork Lumber *(continued)*

(see Sizing Chart on page 9). Most often, the lumber will have been surfaced (milled) on two sides and the edges left rough.

Naturally, the better the grade of wood you order, the more it will cost you. Often, you can save a substantial amount of money by buying the lowest acceptable grade of wood for your project and simply discarding the unusable parts of the board. Ask the sales personnel at the retail outlet for help in selecting the right grade for the project at hand. And

check to make sure you're buying kiln-dried stock; you'll have trouble with unseasoned wood.

When you've decided on a grade, ask a salesperson to figure the number of *board feet*—the standard unit of measurement—you will need to purchase to yield the number of pieces of stock your project requires.

Popular Lumber Species

Species	Characteristics	Relative Cost
Ash (White)	Broad grain pattern, strong, easy to bend, easy to work, tends to split.	Moderate
Birch	Finishes well, can be made to resemble more expensive woods.	Moderate
Genuine Mahogany	Works and finishes well, relatively easy to work.	Moderate
Philippine Mahogany (Red Lauan)	Easy to work, coarse texture, finishes well.	Inexpensive
Maple (Hard)	Most adaptable of all hardwoods, takes stain and works well.	Moderate
Oak (Red & White)	Strong, heavy, finishes well, difficult to shape.	Moderate
Pine	Finishes well, easy to work.	Expensive (Clear Grades)
Poplar	Moderately easy to work, finishes well, fairly weak, doesn't hold nails well.	Inexpensive
Walnut	Strong, durable, works and finishes well, fine grain.	Expensive

Millwork Lumber Grading

Grade	Characteristics
HARDWOODS **First and Seconds (FAS)**	The best grade. Boards usually 6″ and wider, 8′ and longer. Almost clear. Yields 83⅓ percent of clear face cuttings 4″ or wider by 5′ or longer and 3″ or wider by 7′ or longer.
Selects	Boards are 4″ and wider, 6′ and longer. One side is FAS, the other is No. 1 Common. Yields 83⅓ percent clear face cuttings.
No. 1 Common (Thrift Grade)	Boards are 3″ and wider, 4′ and longer. Economical alternative for some uses. Yields 66⅔ percent of clear face cuttings 4″ or wider by 2′ or longer and 3″ or wider by 3′ or longer.
PINE **C Select and Better**	Minor imperfections.
D Select	A few sound defects.
3rd Clear	The best shop grade. Acceptable for cabinets. Well-placed knots allow for high percentage of clear cuts.
No. 1 Shop	More knots and fewer clear cuts than 3rd Clear.
Nos. 2 and 3 Common	The so-called shelving grades. No. 2 has fewer knots than No. 3.

Choosing and Buying Moldings

In the old days, cabinetmakers had to painstakingly carve lumber to make decorative moldings for their projects. Today, that's not necessary with the modern machining techniques being used. You simply decide what kind of molding you want to use, then go to your supplier and place an order for the amount you need. And if you can't find what you're looking for, you can even have moldings specially milled to your specifications.

When shopping for moldings, you'll discover that there are three categories from which to choose: *profile moldings, carved moldings,* and *embossed moldings.* We show examples of each below. Most woodworking specialty catalogs offer a selection of the latter two types, which are sold by the piece.

You can find profile moldings at most building supply outlets. Available in random lengths from 3 to 20 feet, they're made from both softwood (usually pine) and hardwood (usually mahogany, oak, and birch) and are either unfinished or sometimes vinyl-covered.

To estimate your needs, make a list of each piece of molding, and round each measurement up to the next larger foot. Doing this will ensure that you don't come up short of material.

When ordering, keep in mind that you can save money if you'll settle for random lengths purchased on a so-much-per-hundred-linear-feet basis rather than insisting on a specific length. And if you'll be painting the molding, you can save even more by ordering finger-jointed moldings—short pieces that have been joined end to end.

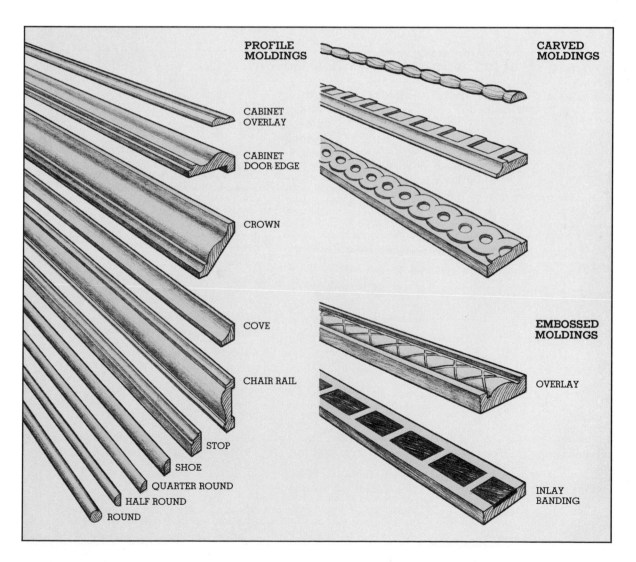

PROFILE MOLDINGS

CABINET OVERLAY

CABINET DOOR EDGE

CROWN

COVE

CHAIR RAIL

STOP

SHOE

QUARTER ROUND

HALF ROUND

ROUND

CARVED MOLDINGS

EMBOSSED MOLDINGS

OVERLAY

INLAY BANDING

Choosing and Buying Sheet Goods

To fashion many of the large components of a cabinet or shelving unit in the "old days," cabinetmakers had no alternative other than edge-joining narrow widths of lumber—an exacting and time-consuming task. Then along came plywood and the other sheet goods. Today, it's difficult to find a project that doesn't use one or more of these useful products. They save valuable time; are widely available, easy to work, and inexpensive compared to their lumber equivalent; and come in quite an array of thicknesses and panel sizes.

The chart below summarizes your sheet goods material options. Note that we've included a couple of items you might not expect to see in a chart of this type—*wood veneer* and *glass*. Wood veneer—actually a thin slice of real wood—allows craftsmen to finish the raw edges of plywood and other sheet goods and to use less-expensive sheet goods as a core material. Some of it comes with an adhesive backing; other types require contact cement.

We've listed three types of glass in the chart—sheet and plate glass and mirror tiles. When ordering glass for your project, jot down the exact size sheets you need and have a glass company do the cutting for you. And be sure to have the edges ground and polished.

Before ordering plywood, particleboard, or hardboard, develop a cutting diagram of the various pieces you need, as discussed on page 34. This is especially important if you're working with hardwood plywood, which can cost $60 or more per sheet. You can't afford to waste any.

What's What in Cabinetmaking Sheet Goods

Material	Grades and Common Types	Thickness (in inches)	Common Panel Sizes (in feet)	Typical Uses
Plywood	Softwood plywood A-A; A-B; A-C A-D	¼; ⅜; ½; ⅝; ¾	2x4; 4x4; 4x8	Projects in which appearance of one or both sides matters—cabinets, drawer fronts, bookcases, built-ins, shelves, tabletops
	MDO	⅜; ¾	4x8	Projects requiring an extra-smooth painting surface—tabletops, cabinets
	Hardwood plywood A-2 (good both sides)	⅛; ¼; ⅜; ½; ¾	2x4; 4x8	Fine furniture and cabinetmaking; decorative wall panels
	G1S (good one side)	⅛; ¼	4x8	
Wood Veneer Available in oak, birch, mahogany, walnut, ash, and others	Strips Slabs	1/32 1/64	13/16" wide 8"x2'; 3'x8'	Finishing exposed edges; veneer work
Particleboard		⅜; ½; ⅝; ¾	2x4; 4x4; 4x8	Core material for laminated furniture and counter tops
Hardboard	Standard; tempered (moisture resistant)	⅛; ¼	2x4; 4x4; 4x8	Underlayment; drawer bottoms and partitions; cabinet backs
Glass	Sheet	⅛; 3/16; ¼	Per order	Cabinet doors
	Plate	⅛; ¼; ⅜; ½	Per order	Shelving
	Mirror tiles	⅛	12"x12"	Cabinet liners

HARDBOARD

PARTICLEBOARD

WOOD VENEER

GLASS

VENEER-CORE
PLYWOOD

PARTICLEBOARD-CORE
PLYWOOD

LUMBER-CORE
PLYWOOD

Choosing and Buying Counter-Top Materials

Not too many years ago, there were very few options when it came to topping off your cabinet projects. But that's definitely not the case today, as you can see on the opposite page. You can choose from a host of materials, including plastic laminate, ceramic tile, laminated wood, cultured and natural marble, and high-density plastic. We discuss each of these here.

Before building any cabinet on which you plan to install a manufactured top, select the top first so you can tailor the size of the cabinet to it. Generally, you'll want the top to overlap the cabinet by one inch at the front and also at the sides (if they don't butt against a wall).

For help with installing plastic laminate and ceramic tile on site-built tops, and for installing any of the manufactured tops, please refer to pages 55-61.

Plastic Laminate

This product, which is actually resin-coated paper that has been laminated under high heat and pressure, comes in two forms—*sheets* and *post-formed* (laminated to a particleboard or plywood backing). Purchase either at most building materials outlets.

Sheet laminate is sold by the square foot and is available in a staggering range of patterns and colors. You may have to special-order the one you want, but delivery usually doesn't take long—a day or two. There's even a new product that has the color impregnated all the way through the sheet material.

This development does away with the unsightly problem of having the laminate's backing show when the laminate is trimmed.

You can buy sheet laminate in two thicknesses—$1/32$ and $1/16$ inch—and in many sizes, from 18x60 inches to 60x144 inches. Buy the thin sheets for vertical applications such as cabinet doors, and the thicker ones for counter tops.

When transporting sheet laminate, loosely roll it (good surface to the inside) and tie it with twine. Also take care to protect the edges of the material, as they are susceptible to damage.

Post-formed tops, which retailers sell by the running foot, typically come in lengths ranging from 4 to 12 feet and in widths of 22 and 25 inches to accommodate both kitchen and vanity cabinets. When ordering one of these, make a diagram of your layout, including any cutouts needed. There's usually an extra charge for any cutting done by the supplier.

Ceramic Tiles

For durability and long-lasting good looks, glazed ceramic tiles can't be beat as a counter-top surface. When shopping for tiles, you'll probably encounter three different types—*individual squares* and other shapes ranging from 1x1 inch on up; *ceramic mosaic tiles,* which come as 1- and 2-inch squares and 1x2-inch rectangles mounted to sheets of paper or mesh; and *pregrouted tiles,* also bonded to sheets, but with flexible, pregrouted joints.

Ask your supplier to suggest the proper adhesive and grout to use for the installation. Check with him, too, about renting tools needed to cut the tiles.

Laminated Wood

Also known as butcher-block, this material is made up of hardwood strips edge-joined together. Though it makes an attractive-looking counter top, laminated wood is quite expensive. It also stains and scratches quite easily. You can pur-

chase the product at most building materials outlets.

Cultured and Natural Marble

Almost everyone loves the look of marble. Considerably fewer people, though, can afford to use it as a counter-top surface. That's why the lower-cost cultured marble tops have been gaining in popularity over the last several years, especially for bathroom vanity situations. Most all of them come with the bowl formed into the top and with the holes for the plumbing fixtures already drilled.

One problem with most cultured marble tops is that they tend to scratch easily. Deep scratches will reveal the core material under the surface.

High-Density Plastic

This material, produced under the trade name Corian®, is another cultured marble product with several positive characteristics. It is durable, resistant to moisture and stains, and easy to keep nice-looking. And because the core material is the same color as the surface, you can get rid of even deep scratches by sanding.

As you might expect, this product is rather expensive. It also demands that you exercise care when working with it, as it can crack.

You can purchase Corian® in sheet form or as one-piece tops and bowls. The sheets come in three thicknesses—$1/4$, $1/2$, and $3/4$ inch; in widths of 25 and 30 inches; and in lengths of up to 12 feet. For more information on the many sizes of one-piece tops available, refer to product literature or ask a supplier.

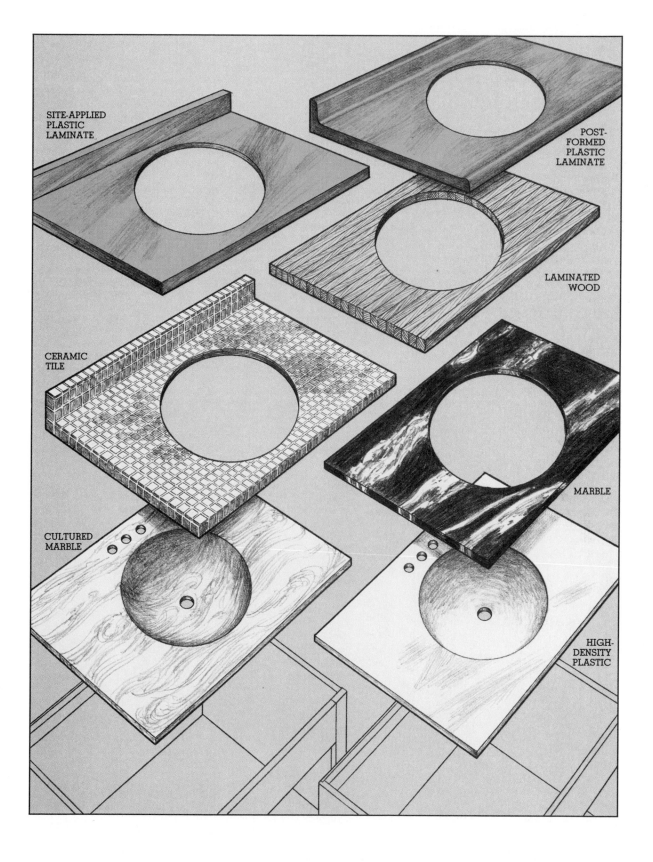

SITE-APPLIED
PLASTIC
LAMINATE

POST-
FORMED
PLASTIC
LAMINATE

LAMINATED
WOOD

CERAMIC
TILE

MARBLE

CULTURED
MARBLE

HIGH-
DENSITY
PLASTIC

Wood-Finishing Materials

Most woodworkers will agree that there is no one "best way" to finish wood. Many simply recommend that the system that works for you is the one to choose. On pages 52-53, we show two systems, one for painting and the other for clear finishing. Here, though, we want to alert you to some of the many products you have available when finishing your cabinet and shelving projects. We've classified them into three separate categories—*abrasives, fillers and sealers,* and *finishes.*

Abrasives

Experienced woodworkers know how vital it is to have a smooth surface prior to finishing. That's why they pay strict attention to the sanding operation. You'll need a supply of garnet sandpaper in grit sizes from 80 (medium) to 220 (extra-fine) for general-purpose sanding, steel wool pads for sanding between finish coats, and if desired, a box each of powdered pumice stone and rottenstone for rubbing out the final finish. And don't forget a tack cloth for removing dust and residue.

Fillers and Sealers

You'll find two types of fillers at your local supplier. Use paste wood filler/sealer to fill the pores and level the surface of open-grain woods prior to applying built-up finishes such as polyurethane varnishes. (If you're applying an oil finish, you don't need this product.)

The products in the other category are designed to cover surface defects and fill nail holes. For painted projects, water putty works well, but with clear-finished projects, you'll need wood putty and possibly

putty sticks that match the color of the stain you've used.

Sealers such as sanding sealer and shellac seal in the stain and fillers, and help prepare the surface for final finishing. (If you use a stain that colors and seals the wood at the same time, you won't need a sealer.)

Finishes

Whether you go with a painted or a clear finish, it does two important things—beautifies and protects the wood. With painted surfaces, you first need to apply a primer to the bare wood. Choose one that's compatible with the type of paint you plan to use. As for paints, you can

use water-, oil-, or alkyd-based formulations. For help with primer and paint selection, check with your paint supplier.

If you choose a clear finish, you have two alternatives—an oil finish or a built-up finish. Oil finishes penetrate, color, and seal the wood as they are applied. No other finishing product need be applied, although you can apply wax or a finish such as polyurethane varnish to further protect the surface.

With built-up finishes, you probably will want to stain the wood first, then use a sealer (if the stain isn't the sealing type), and follow this with several coats of polyurethane varnish or spray lacquer.

Manufactured Shelving and Cabinet Components

Most of the material in this book deals with planning and creating custom-made shelving and cabinet projects. But what if your plans call for an updating of what you have rather than a complete change. Or maybe you can't devote the time needed to build a project. Or maybe the cost of doing what you had initially thought about turned out to be more expense than you can handle right now. If you fall into any of these categories, you may benefit from this page.

Manufacturers know that there's a need for prebuilt cabinets, shelving units, and other components, and they offer a surprisingly wide array of products to satisfy those needs.

Preassembled Unfinished Units

With this type of product, you simply select a piece that's to your liking, then take it home and apply a finish to it. When making your selection, take a close look at how well the unit is constructed. Joints should be tight and well made. Also, note whether it's made of solid or veneered wood. Solid wood furnishings cost substantially more. If you're interested in unfinished units, your best bet for finding a wide selection is to go to a store that specializes in unfinished furniture.

Preassembled Finished Items

With these, simply make your selection, set the unit in the desired location, and if necessary, anchor it to the floor or a wall. You'll find a wide selection exists in every price range.

Ready-to-Assemble Units

Manufacturers of this type of product fabricate all of the project parts, then package the components along with assembly instructions. Offerings run the gamut from metal shelving units all the way to banks of prefinished kitchen cabinets.

Cabinet Face-lift Components

These products are tailor-made for people who want to give their cabinets a new look without buying or building new cabinetry. You can buy ready-to-assemble face frame stock in a variety of wood species, iron-on material that gives a fresh look to older cabinet doors and drawers, and even door and drawer fronts to replace existing ones.

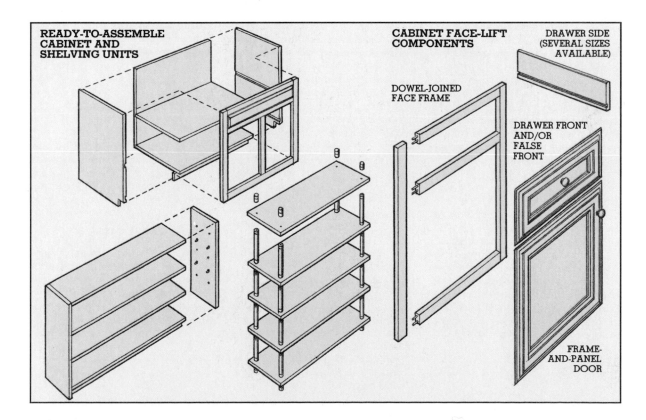

READY-TO-ASSEMBLE CABINET AND SHELVING UNITS

CABINET FACE-LIFT COMPONENTS

DRAWER SIDE (SEVERAL SIZES AVAILABLE)

DOWEL-JOINED FACE FRAME

DRAWER FRONT AND/OR FALSE FRONT

FRAME-AND-PANEL DOOR

Choosing and Buying Hardware

The hardware options available to the cabinetmaker today are phenomenal. There's a fastener for every need, glues and adhesives galore, and shelf supports, cabinet hinges, and accessories of all descriptions. On pages 18-21, we give you a brief rundown of many of the items you'll find at your building supply dealer.

Fasteners

Nails and Screws

No dedicated cabinetmaker would ever be caught without a good supply of nails and screws. The three types of nails shown opposite—brads, finishing nails, and casing nails—are all designed to be set below the surface with a hammer and nail set, then covered with wood putty or dough.

Most often, these nails are pre-packaged rather than sold in bulk. Brads are tiny finishing nails and range in size from ½ to 1½ inches long. Finishing nails come in several lengths—from 1¼ inches (3-penny) to 3 inches (10-penny); casing nails are available from 1½ inches (4-penny) to 3½ inches (16-penny).

To determine the size nail you need for a job, keep in mind that you want one long enough to penetrate well into the lower of the two members being joined.

Wood screws, the type used in cabinetmaking work, are available in plated steel and brass and come with various head shapes (flathead, ovalhead, and roundhead) and slot configurations (single slot and Phillips). Use flatheads when the screw must be flush with or below the sur-face, ovalheads for decorative accent, and roundheads for more utilitarian tasks. Flat and trim washers protect wood surfaces.

As with nails, the right size screw for the job should penetrate well into the lower of the two members being fastened together. When ordering wood screws, specify the *length* (from ¼ to 5 inches), *gauge* or shank diameter (No. 0, which is about $1/16$ inch, to No. 24, about $3/8$ inch), *head type,* and *material.* The larger the screw's gauge (that is, the thicker its shank), the greater its holding power.

Wall Anchors

Sometimes when hanging shelves or securing cabinets, there's no stud into which a screw can be driven. For these situations, and when you're faced with anchoring a project to a concrete wall, wall anchors are the item to turn to for help. If you have a hollow wall and want to fasten something to it, select either a *hollow-wall anchor* or a *toggle bolt.* With both of these fasteners, bore a hole to the diameter specified on the package, then insert the anchor and turn the bolt clockwise. As you can see, as you do so, the flange tightens up against the back side of the wall.

Expansion anchors perform similarly in concrete walls. Again, bore the correct size hole, tap the shield into it, and drive the screw into the shield.

All three of these items come in several sizes and are available at any building materials outlet. The heavier the load, the larger the anchor should be. Note that with hollow-wall anchors, the shank portion must be as long as the wall is thick to work properly.

Glues and Adhesives

Today, cabinetmakers rely less on intricate joinery techniques and more on glues and adhesives to achieve good results. The key is to know when to use which type of product. The following information should help.

Liquid Resin Glue

White glue (polyvinyl resin) and the newer cream-colored glue (aliphatic resin) are both good, general-purpose products for joining components together. The latter sets up more quickly and sands better. Neither is waterproof.

Waterproof (resorcinol) Glue

Use this excellent product if your project requires waterproof joints. With this two-part glue, you must mix the catalyst and the resin exactly as specified on the label directions to get good results. Mix only what you can use immediately.

Contact Cement

Chiefly used in bonding plastic laminate to any of several core materials, contact cement bonds instantly to its mating surface when they touch. Coat both surfaces, allow the cement to dry, then carefully fit the surfaces together. Purchase the non-inflammable, water-based type and be sure to do the work in a well-ventilated area.

Silicone Caulk

This product produces a flexible, waterproof seal at joints of various types, for example, around sinks set in counter tops.

Construction Adhesive

Though formulated especially for installing paneling and other sheet goods, construction adhesive also comes in handy when installing counter tops. Run a bead of it along the top edge of the cabinet, then lower the top onto it.

Shelf Supports

There are literally dozens of hardware items designed to support shelves; only the most common are shown here. See page 25 for information on how to employ these and other support options.

(continued)

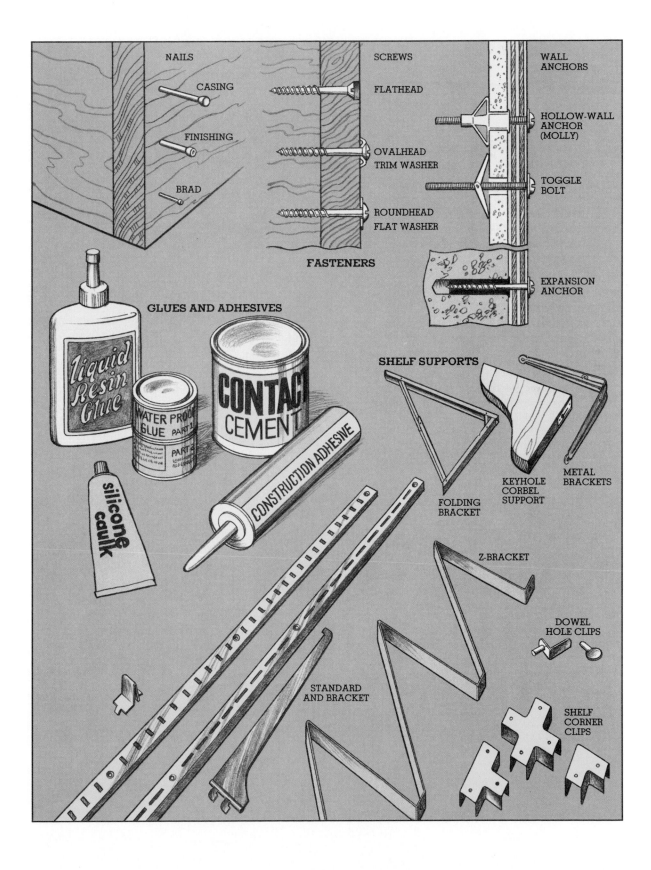

NAILS
CASING
FINISHING
BRAD

SCREWS
FLATHEAD
OVALHEAD
TRIM WASHER
ROUNDHEAD
FLAT WASHER

WALL ANCHORS
HOLLOW-WALL ANCHOR (MOLLY)
TOGGLE BOLT

FASTENERS

EXPANSION ANCHOR

GLUES AND ADHESIVES

liquid Resin Glue

WATER PROOF GLUE PART 1 PART 2

CONTACT CEMENT

CONSTRUCTION ADHESIVE

silicone caulk

SHELF SUPPORTS

KEYHOLE CORBEL SUPPORT

METAL BRACKETS

FOLDING BRACKET

Z-BRACKET

DOWEL HOLE CLIPS

STANDARD AND BRACKET

SHELF CORNER CLIPS

Choosing and Buying Hardware *(continued)*

Door Hinges and Tracks

Early on in the planning stage of your cabinet project, you'll have to decide on the type of doors you want it to have. You have two alternatives—hinged doors and sliding doors. If you choose hinged doors, you must also decide whether you want them to be *lipped, flush,* or *overlapped.* And after choosing one of these, you have to select a hinge that's compatible with that kind of door. To help you with your decision, we have included at right a selection of some commonly used hinges. If you can't find one that appeals to you, pay a visit to your materials supplier and look over his selection of product.

Hinges typically are sold by the *pair.* But for large or extra-heavy doors, you may need a *pair and a half,* or three hinges per door. You can purchase them in a variety of sizes and finishes (usually brass and nickel); all of them come with mounting screws.

Since only very few hinge manufacturers supply installation instructions with their product, be sure to read the information on installing hinges, starting on page 42, before beginning. It can prevent you from making costly and irritating errors.

With sliding doors, there are fewer choices to make. If you want to go without hardware altogether, plow out channels in the cabinet's top and bottom and let the doors slide back and forth in them. Otherwise, you'll need metal or plastic track or vinyl or wooden splines to serve as door guides. For more information on how to install sliding doors, refer to pages 30 and 49.

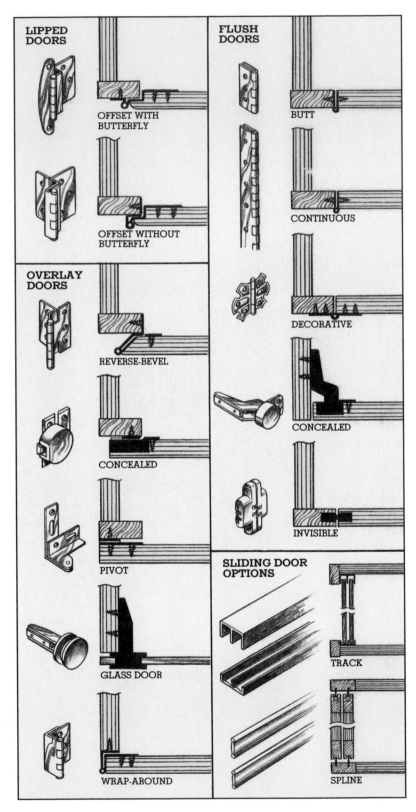

LIPPED DOORS

OFFSET WITH BUTTERFLY

OFFSET WITHOUT BUTTERFLY

OVERLAY DOORS

REVERSE-BEVEL

CONCEALED

PIVOT

GLASS DOOR

WRAP-AROUND

FLUSH DOORS

BUTT

CONTINUOUS

DECORATIVE

CONCEALED

INVISIBLE

SLIDING DOOR OPTIONS

TRACK

SPLINE

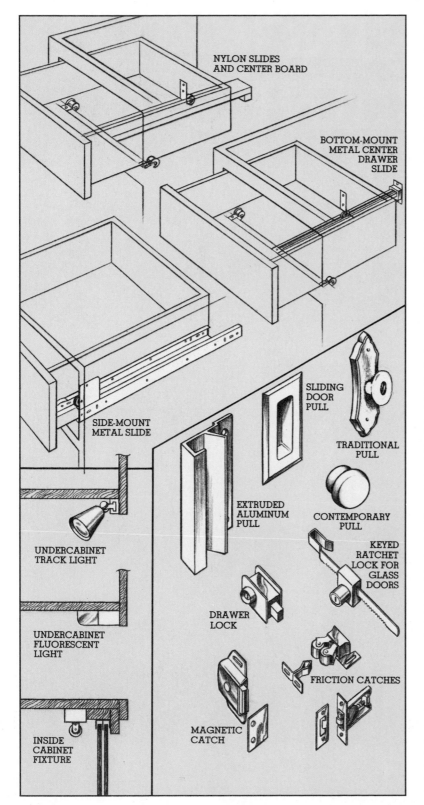

NYLON SLIDES AND CENTER BOARD

BOTTOM-MOUNT METAL CENTER DRAWER SLIDE

SIDE-MOUNT METAL SLIDE

SLIDING DOOR PULL

TRADITIONAL PULL

EXTRUDED ALUMINUM PULL

CONTEMPORARY PULL

KEYED RATCHET LOCK FOR GLASS DOORS

UNDERCABINET TRACK LIGHT

DRAWER LOCK

UNDERCABINET FLUORESCENT LIGHT

FRICTION CATCHES

INSIDE CABINET FIXTURE

MAGNETIC CATCH

Other Cabinet Paraphernalia

Drawer Slides

Of the three types of slides shown at left, the side-mount type is preferred by most cabinetmakers. Though more expensive than the others, it offers longer life and more support. Better quality side-mounts feature ball-bearing rollers and are available in lengths ranging from 12 to 28 inches. Whatever slide type you choose, read the package instructions before installation. They all differ. We show how to install side-mount metal and wooden slides on pages 50-51.

Pulls, Knobs, and Catches

Deciding which pulls or knobs to use for your cabinets is mainly a matter of aesthetics. Most building supply outlets have a wide array of products from which you can choose. But if you're looking for something a bit out of the ordinary, you may have better success looking through special-order catalogs from companies that specialize in cabinet hardware. Your local library should have some of these.

Catches fall into three categories: *friction*, *magnetic*, and *mechanical*. We've included examples of the first two types at left. Both friction and magnetic catches work well for most residential cabinet installations. The mechanical type has fewer residential uses, though childproof safety catches are a notable exception. We show how to install catches on page 48.

Lighting Fixtures

If your plans call for lighting your cabinets, you have several choices. Both the track-type under-cabinet fixture and the under-cabinet fluorescent type cast light down onto work surfaces. For illuminating the inside of a cabinet, as you might with a hutch or curio cabinet, the third fixture shown at left is ideal.

PLANNING GUIDELINES

Regardless of the pursuit, having a plan always pays off—even if you have to alter it along the way. At the very least, you know where you are headed. That's why we spend the next 13 pages showing you what to consider in developing your "project blueprint."

We begin by exploring some of the questions you must answer at the outset of a project, such as what type of unit do you need, will it be a utility item or a piece of furniture, and what style should it be.

Then we turn to the construction options you have with both shelving and cabinets. You'll read about the various types of shelving and shelf support systems, and see charts that will help you determine shelf spans and spacing between shelves. In addition, you'll learn how wall and base cabinets go together, and be exposed to the various cabinet front possibilities, door/drawer style options, common cabinet configurations, and typical cabinet dimensions.

And to help you actually visualize your plan, we show you how to make graph paper drawings and cutting diagrams, as well as how to develop your cutting and materials lists.

First Things First

When architects and design consultants begin working with a client, they start by asking questions designed to find out if the client knows where he or she is headed with the project being considered. Not surprisingly, sometimes the end result differs entirely from what the client originally envisioned.

While you probably don't need an architect's help with your shelving and cabinet needs, you can still pick up valuable tips by considering the following:

What Are Your Needs?
Need more space to house space-consuming items that always seem to be piling up around your place? If so, a few wall-hung shelves or a floor-to-ceiling 2x4 and plywood shelving unit should provide the space quickly and inexpensively.

For dressier storage and display space, consider a freestanding or wall-hung open shelving unit or even a wallful of storage. And if you want a unit with closed storage and the good looks of fine furniture, a cabinet is an excellent choice.

Should the Unit Be Movable or Built In?
Each type has advantages. Many people prefer to build projects they can take with them if they move. With this approach, even large, whole-wall units can be dismantled, if necessary. Built-ins, on the other hand, appear more integrated in the overall room design.

What Materials Should You Use?
Obviously, you want to choose the least expensive material that will do the job. With purely practical units in areas of the home not generally seen by outsiders, shop-grade materials make good economic sense.

Showy projects require better grade materials that, not surprisingly, are more expensive. You can cut project costs somewhat by using lesser-grade goods for parts not exposed to view.

When deciding on materials for furniture-quality units, make sure they complement those used in nearby pieces. For example, if you have an oak dining table and want to build a complementary hutch for the same room, use oak again. This way not only would the grain in the new addition be similar, but your chances of matching finishes would greatly improve.

Finally, keep in mind that the materials you choose will give a certain style to the project. The three examples here point this out very clearly. While nearly identical structurally, visually they're quite different.

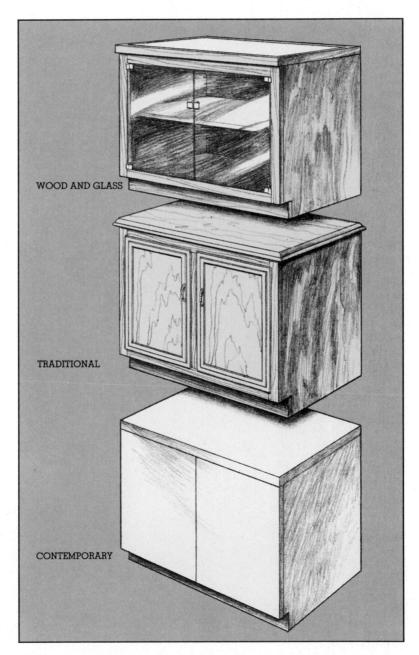

WOOD AND GLASS

TRADITIONAL

CONTEMPORARY

Know Your Construction Options

Shelving

Maybe you need a purely practical place to stash some stuff. Or perhaps it's an attractive showcase for collectibles, knickknacks, or books you want. Whatever your requirements, building a shelving unit is a relatively quick, inexpensive way to satisfy them. And you needn't be a woodworking wizard to produce some dazzling effects of your own—even the first time.

The sketch below classifies shelving into four different categories—*wall-mounted open shelving, floor-to-ceiling open shelving, freestanding enclosed shelving, and stack-able shelving.* Of course, many variations exist within each category. Which you choose depends on your storage and style needs at the time of construction.

Another choice you'll have to make is whether you want *fixed* or *adjustable* shelves. Many people prefer the flexibility afforded by the

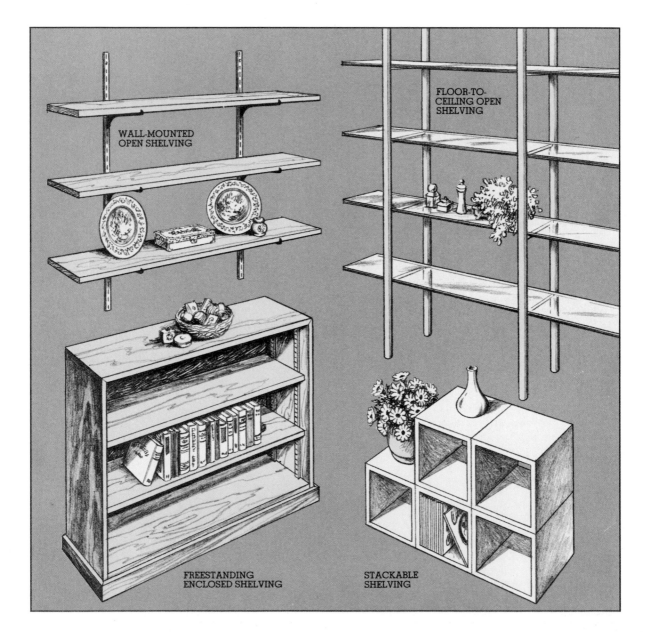

WALL-MOUNTED
OPEN SHELVING

FLOOR-TO-
CEILING OPEN
SHELVING

FREESTANDING
ENCLOSED SHELVING

STACKABLE
SHELVING

latter. The sketch below shows several ways to build either type.

For the shelves themselves, choose from plywood, particleboard, solid lumber, acrylic, or glass. Refer to the Shelving Spans and Shelf Spacing charts at right for help in determining the optimum distance horizontally between shelving supports and vertically between shelves. For items not listed, allow an inch or more clearance between the top of the object and the next higher shelf.

Shelving Spans

Material Used	Maximum Span
¾-inch plywood	36″
¾-inch particleboard	28″
1x12 lumber	24″
2x10 or 2x12 lumber	48-56″
½-inch acrylic	22″
⅜-inch glass	18″

(Assumes shelves fully loaded with books)

Shelf Spacing

Item	Space Required
Paperback books	8″
Hardback books	11″
Oversized hardbacks	15″
Catalog-format books	15½″
Record albums	13¼″
Cassette tapes	5″
Circular slide trays	9¾″

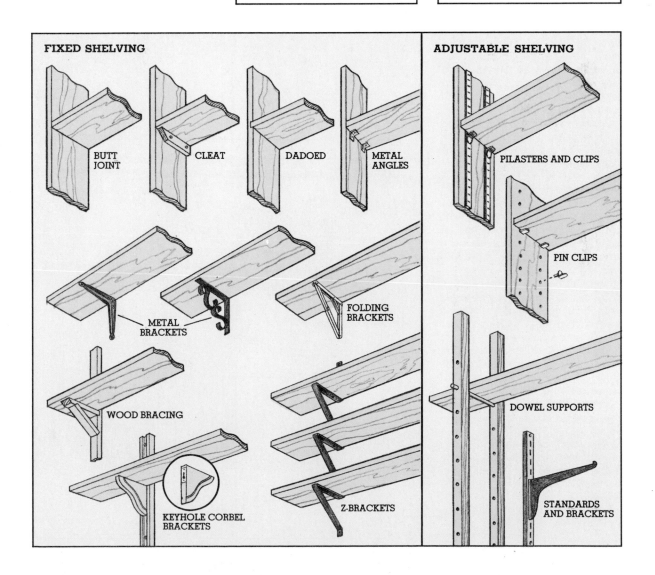

FIXED SHELVING

BUTT JOINT
CLEAT
DADOED
METAL ANGLES
METAL BRACKETS
FOLDING BRACKETS
WOOD BRACING
KEYHOLE CORBEL BRACKETS
Z-BRACKETS

ADJUSTABLE SHELVING

PILASTERS AND CLIPS
PIN CLIPS
DOWEL SUPPORTS
STANDARDS AND BRACKETS

Cabinets

Cabinetmakers know it. So do architects and others in the building field. But if you've never built a cabinet before, you may not realize that you needn't be a master craftsman to fashion a good-looking, solidly built project yourself.

On the next six pages, we show you some of the options you have when building kitchen cabinets and vanities. And even if the project you have in mind is more furniture oriented—a hutch, dresser, end table, or desk, for example—you'll find the information quite helpful.

The Carcass

Behind every good-looking cabinet front you'll find a *carcass,* or frame, made of edge-joined stock, plywood, or framing lumber sheathed with plywood. As you can see at right, we've chosen to use plywood panels.

Though we show two anatomies for you to study—a *base cabinet* and a *wall cabinet*—there aren't many differences in the way they're constructed. In each case, ¾-inch plywood panels form the perimeter of the cabinet, ¼-inch plywood encloses it at the back, and a dowel-joined face frame of solid lumber ties the unit together at the front and serves as the frame for doors and drawers.

Note that the base cabinet rests on a frame that creates necessary *toespace* at the front of the cabinet. The notch in the front frame member allows the notched side panels to fit flush against the unit and hide the exposed plywood edge for a finished appearance. The *ledger* at the back of the cabinet provides a solid surface through which screws are driven to anchor the unit to the wall.

With wall cabinets you don't need a base, but you will need a ledger at the top and bottom, again as a surface for securing the unit to the wall.

For more about constructing cabinet carcasses, see pages 37-39.

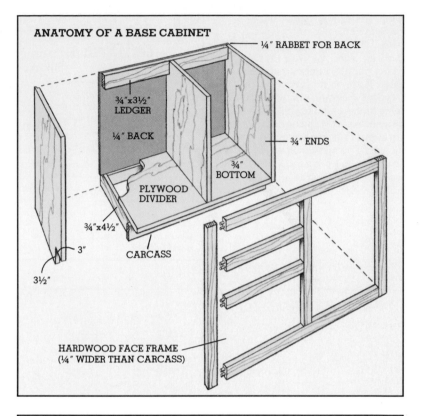

ANATOMY OF A BASE CABINET

¼" RABBET FOR BACK
¾"x3½" LEDGER
¼" BACK
¾" ENDS
¾" BOTTOM
PLYWOOD DIVIDER
¾"x4½"
3"
3½"
CARCASS
HARDWOOD FACE FRAME (¼" WIDER THAN CARCASS)

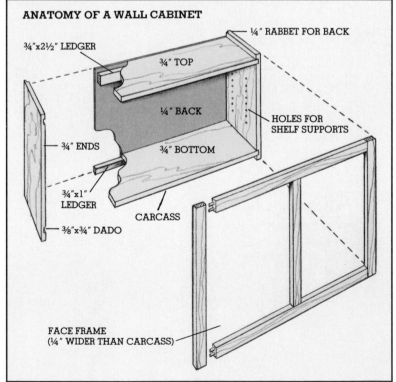

ANATOMY OF A WALL CABINET

¾"x2½" LEDGER
¼" RABBET FOR BACK
¾" TOP
¼" BACK
HOLES FOR SHELF SUPPORTS
¾" ENDS
¾" BOTTOM
¾"x1" LEDGER
CARCASS
⅜"x¾" DADO
FACE FRAME (¼" WIDER THAN CARCASS)

Cabinet Front Possibilities

You add personality to a cabinet when you fit it with doors and drawers. In shaping this personality, there are several things to consider.

First, choose the *type* doors and drawers you want—*lipped, flush,* or *overlay.* (Whichever you choose, we'll show you the hinging options.) Select a *style—traditional* or *contemporary*—and the *configuration* of the cabinet—how many doors and drawers and in what arrangement. All of these considerations are explained on this and the following four pages.

Lipped Doors and Drawers

As the name implies, this construction features doors and drawers with rabbeted edges overlapping each edge of the opening. Typically, the doors and drawer fronts are cut ½ inch wider and longer than the opening, then rabbeted so that the lip rests flush with the face frame.

Offset hinges, with or without a butterfly (a flange), secure the doors to the face frame. The self-closing type is best.

The exploded-view drawing of the drawer below reveals a ¾-inch drawer front, ½-inch sides and back, and a ¼-inch bottom that fits into dadoes in the front and sides.

The back sits atop the bottom and between the rabbeted sides. Here, as in the other constructions, we show metal slides being used, mainly because they offer durability and ease of operation. Note, also, that the front is rabbeted to accept the sides and metal slides and still overlap the face frame.

You must construct the drawer no less than 1 inch narrower than the face frame opening to make way for the drawer slides, and ¼ inch shorter than the height of the opening. Drawer depth, however, is a matter of personal preference.

(continued)

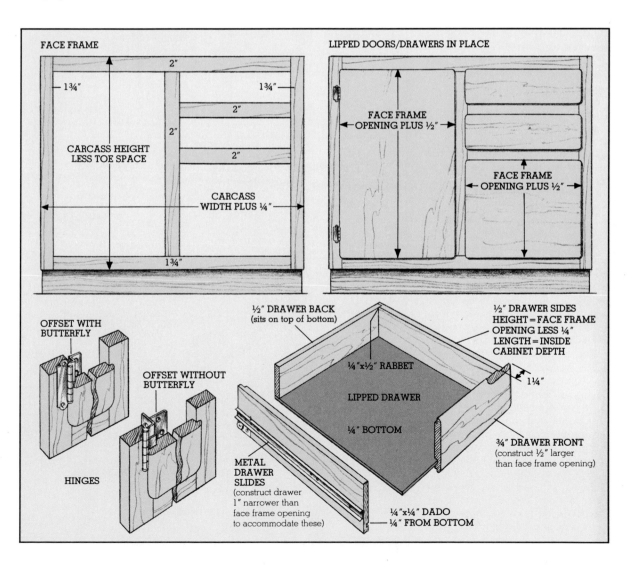

FACE FRAME

2"
1¾"
2"
2"
1¾"
2"
CARCASS HEIGHT LESS TOE SPACE
CARCASS WIDTH PLUS ¼"
1¾"

LIPPED DOORS/DRAWERS IN PLACE

FACE FRAME OPENING PLUS ½"
FACE FRAME OPENING PLUS ½"

OFFSET WITH BUTTERFLY
OFFSET WITHOUT BUTTERFLY
HINGES

½" DRAWER BACK (sits on top of bottom)
¼"x½" RABBET
LIPPED DRAWER
¼" BOTTOM

½" DRAWER SIDES HEIGHT = FACE FRAME OPENING LESS ¼" LENGTH = INSIDE CABINET DEPTH
1¼"
¾" DRAWER FRONT (construct ½" larger than face frame opening)

METAL DRAWER SLIDES (construct drawer 1" narrower than face frame opening to accommodate these)
¼"x¼" DADO ¼" FROM BOTTOM

Cabinet Front
Possibilities *(continued)*

Flush Doors and Drawers

If your tastes lean toward the contemporary, you'll probably be interested in flush doors and drawers. (Flush here means flush with the face frame surface.) Be advised, though, that these are the most difficult of the three hinged door options to position in the frame opening.

In the sketch at right, we show two face frame situations from which to choose. If you prefer uniform spacing around the doors and drawers, construct the face frame as shown in the first example. Otherwise, you can dispense with the bottom portion of the face frame and cut the doors and drawers so they cover the bottom shelf of the cabinet.

To the right of each of the face frames, note that we've included formulas for determining the correct dimensions of doors and drawers. What you'll end up with is about a $1/16$-inch space between the door or drawer and the face frame.

NOTE: If using plastic laminate as a finish material, be sure to factor in its thickness.

With flush doors, you have several hinge options. Which you decide on depends on what look you want. Choose from butt, invisible (both shown here), decorative, inset, and concealed hinges. You can learn how to install all of them on pages 44-45. Butt and decorative hinges are the easiest to install; invisible, the most difficult. Many prefer concealed hinges because they are unobtrusive and self-closing.

Flush drawers go together in very much the same way lipped doors do. Note, though, that instead of having a rabbeted drawer front, flush drawers have two front members: one that fits between the rabbeted sides, and another that screws onto the drawer. One advantage of this construction is that if you decide to change the looks of your cabinets, you can simply screw another drawer front to the drawer. Too, only the front piece needs to be of cabinet-quality stock.

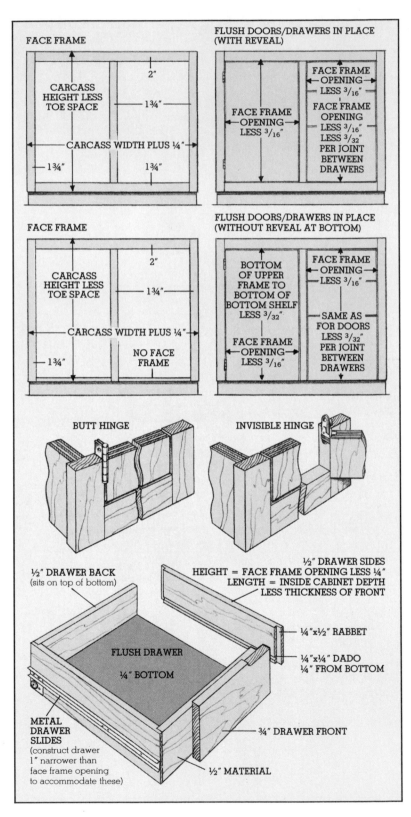

An overwhelming majority of kitchen and vanity cabinets commercially produced, and many of the custom-made ones, have *overlay* doors and drawers. Why? They offer clean, good looks and allow for more adjustment flexibility during installation. Even if your measurements are slightly off, you can still achieve professional-looking results by making minor adjustments.

Another type, the *full-overlay*, completely covers the face frame. Though not nearly as easy to install as the overlay, they, too, give cabinets a crisp, well-ordered appearance. For help with determining the dimensions of the door and drawer fronts, refer to the sketch at right.

For hinging these doors, several options exist. With full-overlay doors, choose from pivot (shown), offset, and concealed hinges. If you decide on overlay doors, self-closing or concealed hinges (shown) are best. For installation pointers for all of these types, see pages 46-47.

Drawers with overlay fronts are constructed much the same way as those with flush fronts. (See the exploded-view drawing at right for details.) The only real difference is the size you cut the drawer fronts.

Glass or Plastic Hinged Doors

Sometimes you want the items stored in a cabinet to be seen, as in a hutch or even wall-mounted kitchen cabinets. For situations like these, or if you just want something a bit different from what everyone else has, plastic or glass doors are a logical choice. You can combine either with a wood frame, and hang the door as discussed on pages 27-29, or let the doors stand alone as is done on page 30.

If you prefer the look of flush doors, size them so there's a ⅛-inch clearance all around. With overlay doors, plan for a ¼-inch overlap of the face frame. *(continued)*

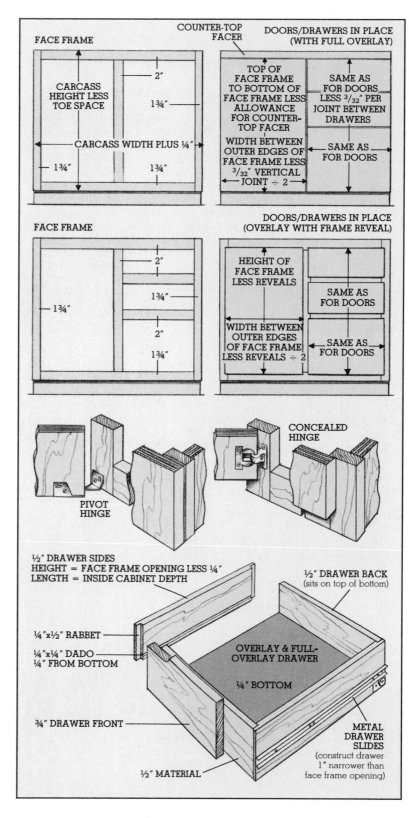

Cabinet Front Possibilities *(continued)*

Note the hinges used with each of these types of doors. The hinge holding the flush door in place does so with pressure that's exerted by set-screws. After you mount two of these hinges to the cabinet, fit the glass or plastic into the hinges' channels.

Unlike the hinge just discussed, the one used with the overlap door requires that you have holes cut in the glass to accept the barrel portion of the hinge. Before ordering glass or plastic doors, read the instructions accompanying the hinges to find the location of the holes. It's usually advisable to have these holes cut by a supplier who does this sort of thing regularly.

Sliding Doors

Rather than being supported by a pair of hinges, sliding cabinet doors glide in or on channels fastened to or recessed into the cabinet's top and bottom shelves. Their drawback is that you only have access to one side of the cabinet at a time.

The sketch below depicts two typical sliding door situations. In the first example, the cabinet's face frame neatly conceals the aluminum track in which the doors travel.

Here, the track is fastened to spacer blocks that are attached to the cabinet's top and bottom shelves, but if you'd rather, you can recess the track into dadoes cut into the cabinet. The doors for this installation should be $1/16$ inch shorter than the distance between the top of the upper track and the top of the lower one. Also, make each door $\frac{1}{2}$ inch wider than half of the distance between the inner edges of the cabinet sides.

If you choose vinyl splines, as in the second example, size the doors according to the guidelines below.

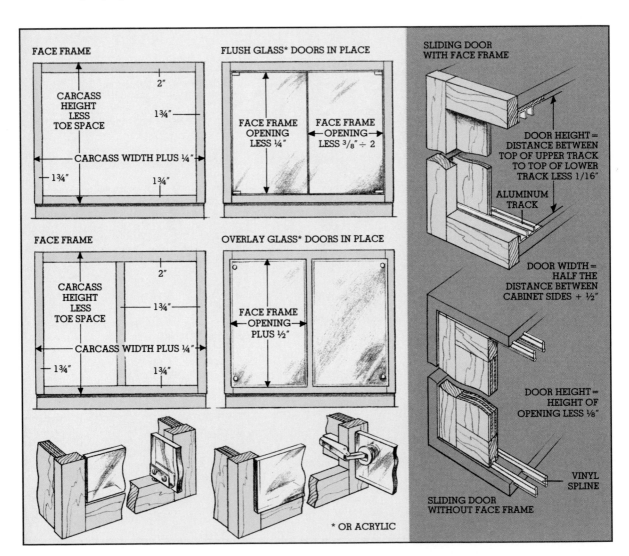

FACE FRAME

CARCASS HEIGHT LESS TOE SPACE

2"

1¾"

1¾"

CARCASS WIDTH PLUS ¼"

1¾"

FACE FRAME

CARCASS HEIGHT LESS TOE SPACE

2"

1¾"

1¾"

CARCASS WIDTH PLUS ¼"

1¾"

FLUSH GLASS* DOORS IN PLACE

FACE FRAME OPENING LESS ¼"

FACE FRAME OPENING LESS ³/₈" ÷ 2

OVERLAY GLASS* DOORS IN PLACE

FACE FRAME OPENING PLUS ½"

SLIDING DOOR WITH FACE FRAME

DOOR HEIGHT = DISTANCE BETWEEN TOP OF UPPER TRACK TO TOP OF LOWER TRACK LESS 1/16"

ALUMINUM TRACK

DOOR WIDTH = HALF THE DISTANCE BETWEEN CABINET SIDES + ½"

DOOR HEIGHT = HEIGHT OF OPENING LESS ⅛"

VINYL SPLINE

SLIDING DOOR WITHOUT FACE FRAME

* OR ACRYLIC

Door/Drawer Style Options

As you can see in the sketch at right, there's no shortage of cabinet door and drawer styles from which to select. Actually, hundreds of variations exist; however, they all fall into one of two categories—*slab* or *frame and panel*.

If you decide on the slab type, use ¾-inch panels to ensure adequate stability. Thinner stock doesn't hold up to the rigors doors and drawers are subject to. Glass doors are the only exception to this; typically, they're ¼ inch thick. As for styling slab doors and drawers, you can leave them plain, rout designs into them, or add moldings to their surface (see sketch). The style of the drawers should match the style of the doors.

With frame and panel doors, the frame supplies the needed strength, so you can go with thinner panels, fabric, or other inserts. Generally, these are set into rabbets cut into the back side of the frame. Be sure to style the drawer fronts so they're compatible with the doors; realize, though, that they'll have to be solid rather than frame and panel.

Common Cabinet Configurations

How you divide up the space in your cabinet depends on its size and intended use. Cabinets up to 24 inches wide generally have one door and sometimes a drawer or false drawer front above it, or a bank of drawers, and no doors. With cabinets wider than 24 inches, you can select a couple of doors, a door and a bank of drawers, or any of several other combinations.

An important reminder—be sure to keep doors and drawers in vertical and horizontal alignment. Doing this will yield a cabinet that's as eye-catching as it is functional.

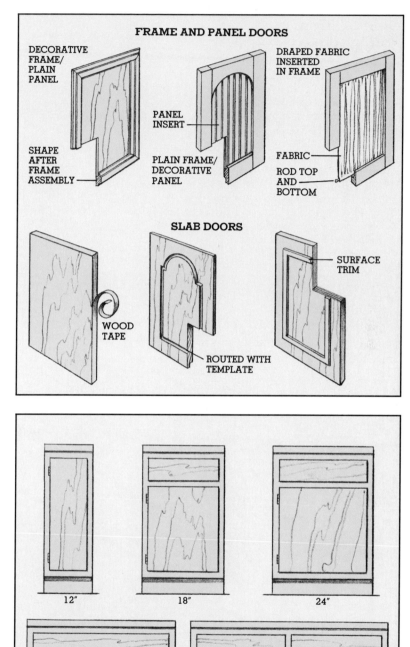

Typical Dimensions

Before you can commit your cabinetry plan to paper, which we advise you to do on pages 34-35, you need to decide on the unit's overall dimensions. While you have some flexibility here, you'll want to stay fairly close to the standard dimensions found on these two pages. Experience has shown that they work well in most situations.

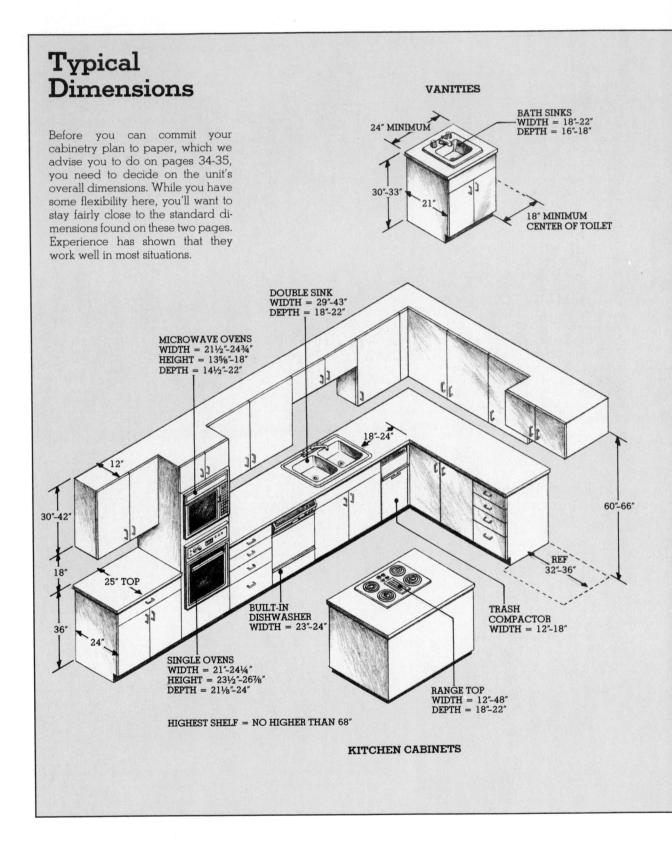

VANITIES

BATH SINKS
WIDTH = 18"-22"
DEPTH = 16"-18"

24" MINIMUM

30"-33"

21"

18" MINIMUM
CENTER OF TOILET

DOUBLE SINK
WIDTH = 29"-43"
DEPTH = 18"-22"

MICROWAVE OVENS
WIDTH = 21½"-24¾"
HEIGHT = 13⅝"-18"
DEPTH = 14½"-22"

18"-24"

60"-66"

12"

30"-42"

18"

25" TOP

36"

24"

REF
32"-36"

TRASH
COMPACTOR
WIDTH = 12"-18"

SINGLE OVENS
WIDTH = 21"-24¼"
HEIGHT = 23½"-26⅞"
DEPTH = 21⅛"-24"

BUILT-IN
DISHWASHER
WIDTH = 23"-24"

RANGE TOP
WIDTH = 12"-48"
DEPTH = 18"-22"

HIGHEST SHELF = NO HIGHER THAN 68"

KITCHEN CABINETS

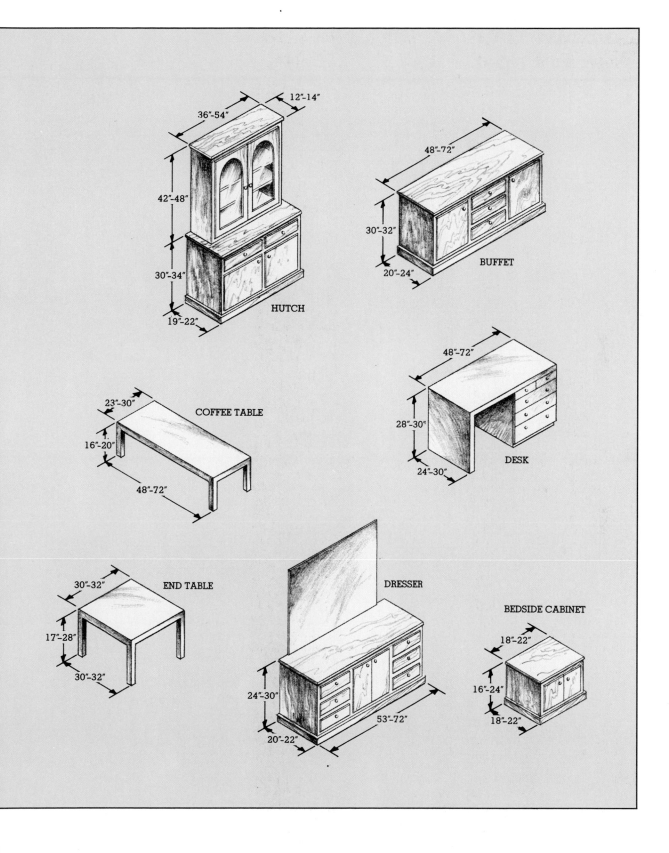

Commit Your Plan to Paper

Without a road map, finding your way around in an unfamiliar city is almost impossible. So is building a cabinet without a detailed plan in front of you. Even professional cabinetmakers take the time necessary to dimension all of a cabinet's components before making the first cut. Why? Because even minor measurement or cutting errors will detract from the looks of a project—and cost money.

Committing your plan to paper involves several things. First, using graph paper, draw three *scaled sketches* of your project—a front view, an end view, and a top view—noting the dimensions of each member. Draw detailed sketches of any areas with construction oddities. Recheck all of the dimensions for accuracy. (The drawings below and on the following page are for a vanity cabinet that measures 38 inches wide, 22 inches deep, and 30 inches high.)

Next, make a *cutting list* like the one we made for this project. Notice that the list is divided by the type of lumber used—¾-inch hardwood, ¾-inch framing lumber, ¾-inch plywood, and ¼-inch plywood. A further breakdown of the materials needed under each type of lumber helps categorize the components of each subassembly. For best results, discipline yourself to be specific.

Then make the *cutting diagrams* of the various components using graph paper. Doing this will help you determine how much of each material you need to buy. Remem-

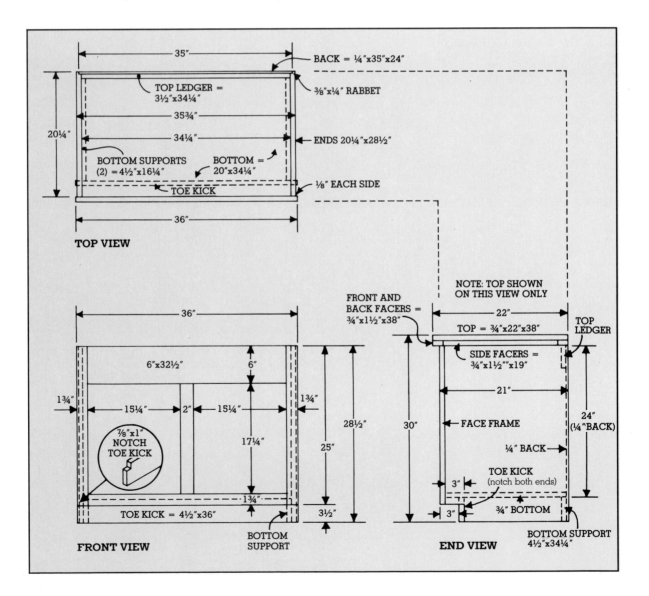

TOP VIEW

BACK = ¼"x35"x24"
TOP LEDGER = 3½"x34¼"
⅜"x¼" RABBET
35¾"
34¼"
20¼"
ENDS 20¼"x28½"
BOTTOM SUPPORTS (2) = 4½"x16¼"
BOTTOM = 20"x34¼"
⅛" EACH SIDE
TOE KICK
36"
35"

FRONT VIEW

36"
6"x32½"
6"
1¾"
15¼"
2"
15¼"
1¾"
⅞"x1" NOTCH TOE KICK
17¼"
28½"
25"
1¾"
TOE KICK = 4½"x36"
3½"
BOTTOM SUPPORT

END VIEW

FRONT AND BACK FACERS = ¾"x1½"x38"
NOTE: TOP SHOWN ON THIS VIEW ONLY
22"
TOP = ¾"x22"x38"
TOP LEDGER
SIDE FACERS = ¾"x1½""x19"
21"
FACE FRAME
24" (¼"BACK)
¼" BACK
30"
TOE KICK (notch both ends)
3"
3"
¾" BOTTOM
BOTTOM SUPPORT 4½"x34¼"

ber to consider grain direction when positioning members on plywood panels. You will want the grain of the side panels, for example, to be running the same direction. Also, when laying out any of the components, be sure to figure in the amount of material that will be lost to the saw blade.

Finally, you'll need a *materials list* to take to your materials supplier. Jot down your lumber needs as well as the miscellaneous items such as hinges, nails, etc. You also may find it helpful to take your sketches and cutting list with you.

Cutting List

¾" Hardwood

Face Frame	6"x32½"
	2"x17¼"
	1¾"x32½"
	1¾"x25"
	1¾"x25"
Toe Kick	4½"x36"

¾" Framing Lumber

Top Ledger	3½"x34¼"
Bottom Support	4½"x34¼"
Side Supports	4½"x16¼"
	4½"x16¼"

¾" Plywood

Ends	20¼"x28½"
	20¼"x28½"
Top	22"x38"
Bottom	20"x34¼"
Doors	15¾"x17¾"
	15¾"x17¾"
Front Facer	1½"x38"
Back Facer	1½"x38"
Side Facers	1½"x19"
	1½"x19"

¼" Plywood

| Back | 24"x35" |

Materials List

1 Piece Hardwood ¾"x7"x8'
1 Piece Framing ¾"x5"x9'
   Lumber
1 Sheet Plywood 48"x96"x¾"
1 Sheet Plywood 24"x48"x¼"
2 Pairs Self-Closing
   Hinges
2 Pulls
Nails
Glue
Stain
Sealer
Plastic Laminate
Contact Cement

CUTTING DIAGRAM

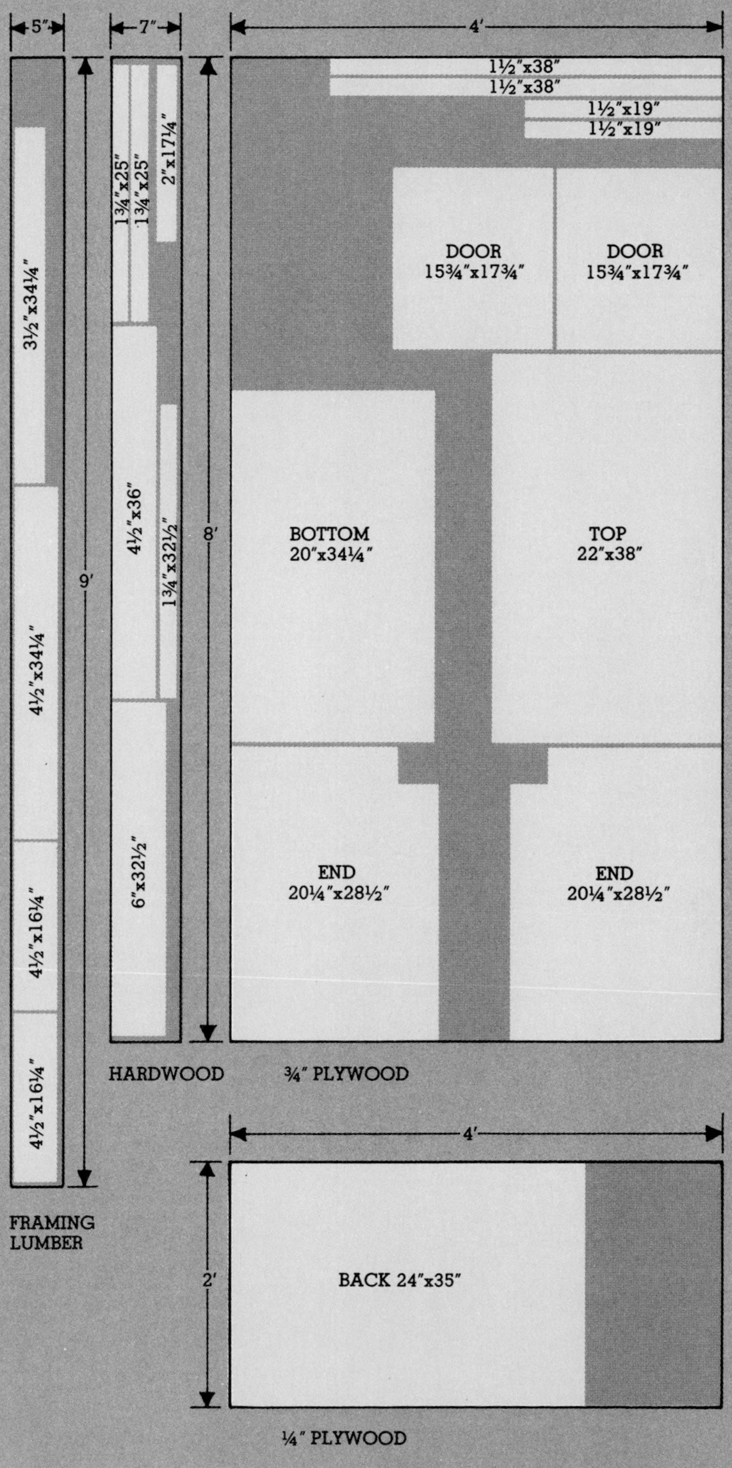

THE ABC's OF CABINET CONSTRUCTION

In Chapter 1, you learned about the materials and hardware available for making cabinets and shelves. And in Chapter 2, we walked you through the steps involved in planning your project.

Now comes the exciting part—assembling and finishing your project. As you're about to find out, cabinet construction is a process that's not nearly as complex as you might have thought. We begin by showing you how to assemble the cabinet shell, or *carcass,* and how to fasten the face frame to it.

Next, you'll read about three ways to install shelves and learn how to install hinged and sliding doors, as well as drawers and false cabinet fronts.

Applying a finish to the project—either paint or a clear finish—comes next, followed by instructions on cabinet installation.

And because no base cabinet is complete without a counter top, we conclude the chapter by showing you how to install several different types of tops.

The cabinets we show in various stages of construction in this chapter are the popular kitchen/vanity type. For more project ideas, plans, and step-by-step instructions, see the "Project Potpourri" chapter beginning on page 78.

Assembling the Cabinet Shell

Base Cabinets

1 Start by cutting the base pieces to the sizes specified in your plan. (For help with planning your project and committing that plan to paper, refer to the "Planning Guidelines" chapter beginning on page 22.) Then, using woodworkers' glue and 6d or 8d finishing nails with your material on a flat surface, join the members together. Be sure to align the sides with the notched front piece as shown in sketch 1.

Now, using a framing square, check the base for square. If it's a bit off, nudge it into position with your hammer. If it's way off, recheck your measurements. You might have to do some trimming.

2 Cut the cabinet sides to size, notch the front edge of each so it will fit over the notch in the front base member, and rabbet the back edge of each side to accommodate the cabinet back. (For information on how to make rabbet cuts, see the "Cutting and Joining Techniques" chapter beginning on page 62.) Glue and nail the sides to the base.

To ensure a good bond, tip the unit on its back and clamp the sides and base together, using a pair of pipe clamps and a couple of pieces of scrap wood to equalize the pressure being exerted.

3 After allowing the glue to set up for the time specified on the container label, remove the clamps and return the cabinet to its upright position. Then cut the bottom shelf to size and test-fit it between the cabinet sides. Be sure to position the shelf so it is flush with the front of the sides. If it fits correctly, run a wavy bead of glue along the top edge of the base members, set the shelf in place, and secure it with finishing nails. *(continued)*

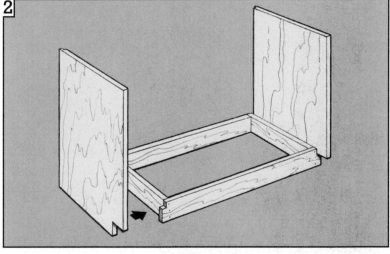

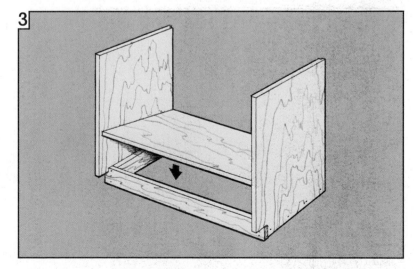

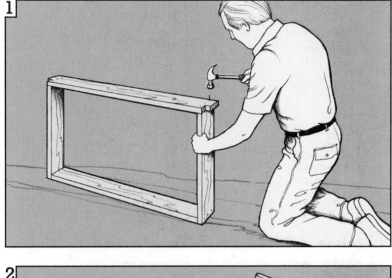

Base Cabinets *(continued)*

4 Before cutting the ledger, double-check its length by measuring the distance between the inside edges of the cabinet sides. (Cutting the ledger to this dimension ensures a square opening for the cabinet back to fit into.) Now, position the ledger between the sides as shown and drill pilot holes through the sides and into the ledger. Remove the ledger to apply glue, then secure it by driving in finishing nails.

5 (If the unit you are building has shelves supported by stopped dadoes, insert them into the cabinet shell now; you can't do it after the back goes on.) Cut the cabinet back to size, then prior to positioning it, drive several finishing nails partway through it near the edges. Now lay a bead of adhesive in the rabbet on both sides and secure the back.

6 If your plan includes one or more vertical dividers to compartmentalize space within the cabinet, cut the panel(s) so its front edge aligns with the cabinet sides and bottom shelf, and its top edge aligns with the side panels' top edges. And don't forget to cut a notch at the top back edge so the divider will fit in around the ledger.

Where you position the divider(s) depends on the configuration of the interior space of the cabinet. If yours will have two doors and no drawers, fasten the divider midway between the sides. But if you've opted for a door and a bank of drawers, you'll want it off-center enough so that when the face frame is attached, the divider will serve as the surface for the drawer slide.

Run a bead of glue along the back and bottom edges of the divider and nail it into place from the back and bottom of the cabinet. If you prefer, you can fit the divider in place at this point and secure it after you've attached the face frame (see page 40).

If your cabinet has shelves supported by full dadoes, insert and secure them now.

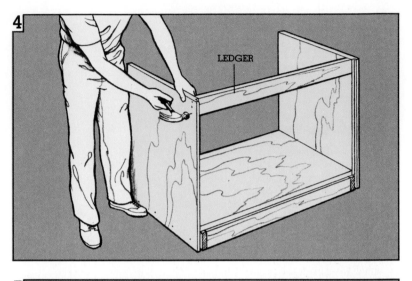

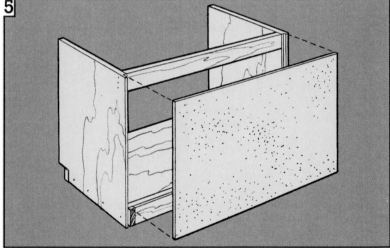

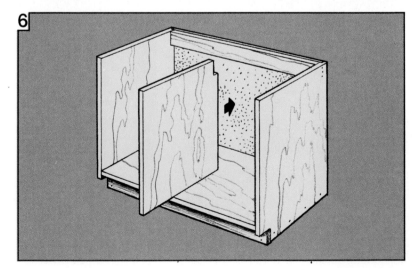

Wall Cabinets

1 Start by cutting the top, bottom, and sides to the size specified in your project plan. (For help with planning your project, see the "Planning Guidelines" chapter beginning on page 22. And for information on making various cuts, refer to the "Cutting and Joining Techniques" chapter, beginning on page 62.) Don't forget to rabbet the back edge of each side to accept the cabinet back and to cut dadoes for the top and bottom shelves. You may also want to cut grooves or drill holes in the sides at this time if you plan to support shelves with recessed pilasters or shelf clips (see pages 41-42).

Now, glue and nail the frame together. To ensure a good, tight fit, use a couple of pipe clamps and wood scraps to apply pressure to the unit. (See the glue container to determine the proper curing time.)

2 Cut top and bottom ledgers to length, then glue and nail them to the cabinet as shown.

3 Cut the cabinet back to size, then lay the shell facedown, and glue and nail the back as shown.

4 Cut any dividers to size, notch the top back edge to fit around the top ledger, and glue and nail in place. Use a square to confirm that the divider is square with the shelves.

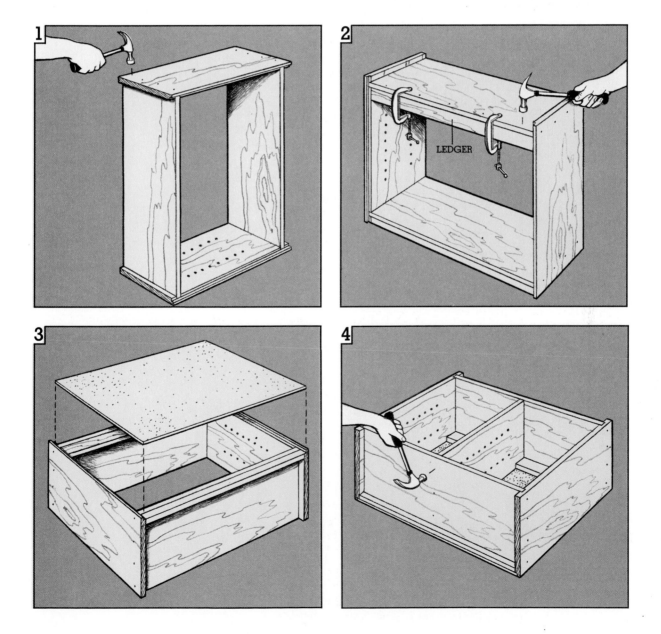

Attaching the Face Frame

1 With the cabinet on its back, apply glue and spread it along the front edge of the sides and top and bottom shelves.

2 If you joined the face frame members with dowels (discussed on page 77) or preassembled the face frame using butt or lap joints, apply glue to the backside of the face frame, then position and nail the frame to the cabinet every eight inches with 6d finishing nails. (The top of the upper face frame member should align with the top of the sides; the top of the lower member, with the top of the bottom shelf. On cabinets with sliding doors, the top of the lower member should be flush with the top of the track.) Clamp the face frame to the cabinet (see pages 75-77).

3 If you nail on the members separately, secure the side members first, then clamp the rails between the sides and nail the members together. Now, clamp the face frame to the cabinet (see pages 75-77).

4 Recess the nails on the face frame and elsewhere on the cabinet.

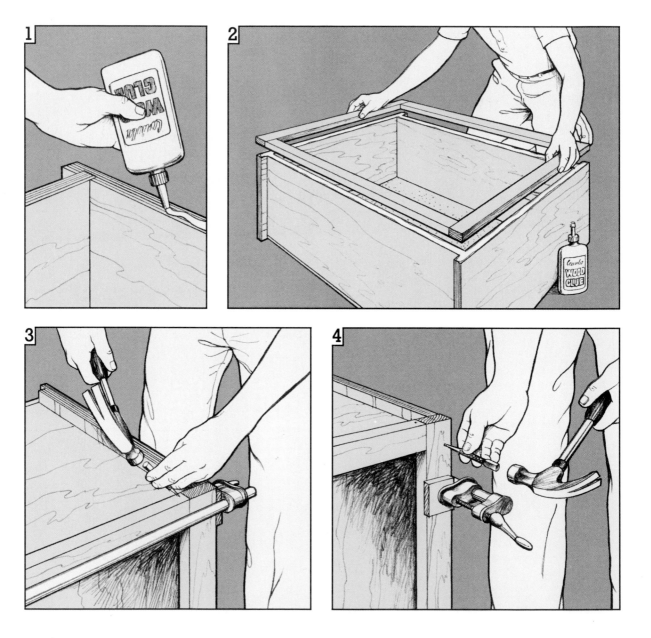

Adding Shelves to Cabinets

Basically, you have four major shelf support options to consider when building cabinets. With adjustable shelves, choose from pilasters and clips, and pins or dowels that fit into dowel holes. If you want fixed shelves, you need to decide between ledgers and butt joints.

On pages 41-43, we show you how to install all but the butt-joint shelving. With the latter type, simply decide where on the uprights to locate the shelves, then either cut dadoes for the shelves to slip into or butt the shelves directly against the surface of the sides. (If you choose this method, install the shelves while you're assembling the shell—see pages 37-39.)

Keep in mind that if you decide on plywood or particleboard shelves for your unit, you'll need to cover their front edges and sometimes their end edges in one of the three ways shown in the top sketch. *Wood filler* works well if you plan to paint the shelves. For clear-finished cabinets or shelving units, use either *wood molding* or *wood edge tape*.

Fastening Shelf Cleats to a Cabinet Shell

1 Make a mark (on either upright) at each point where you want the *top* of a shelf. Then, using a combination square as shown, strike a line at each point.

2 Now, hold each cleat in position with one hand and drill a pair of holes through the cleat and into the upright. Glue and nail each cleat in place. Repeat this same procedure for the other upright.

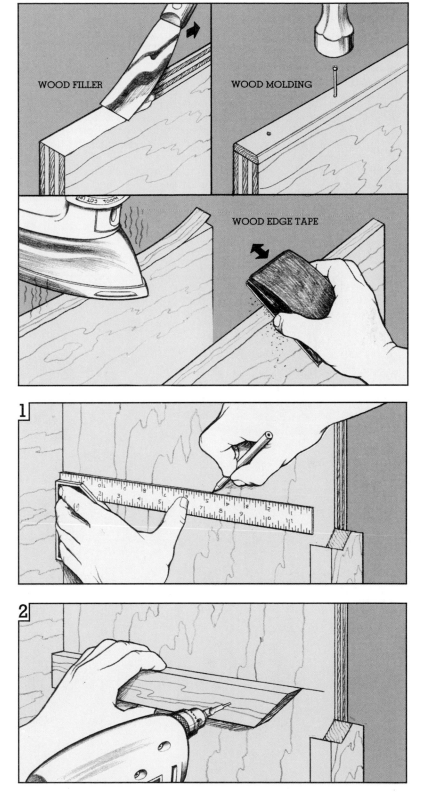

WOOD FILLER

WOOD MOLDING

WOOD EDGE TAPE

1

2

Adding Shelves to Cabinets *(continued)*

Fastening Pilasters to a Cabinet Shell

1 Measure the distance between the top of the bottom shelf and the bottom of the top shelf (or the top edge of the cabinet side). Now lay a pair of pilasters side by side, with the numbers and hash marks lined up, and mark the cutoff line. Cut them to length with a hacksaw. Use either of these as a pattern to cut enough pilasters to satisfy your needs, again making sure that the numbers and hash marks line up. (The numbers and hash marks will help you correctly position the clips used to support the shelves.)

2 (If your unit has recessed pilasters, you can skip this step, as you would already have made the dado cuts in the cabinet sides.) Now, mark the location of the pilasters. Make a light pencil mark near the top and bottom of the cabinet sides, and if you have mid-support, also on the back side of the middle face frame stile. (In most situations, you'll want the pilasters that support the ends of the shelves positioned about an inch in from the front and back edges of the shelves.) Connect your marks, using one of the pilasters as a straightedge.

3 If your unit has recessed pilasters, place each strip into a recess and mark the location of the screws that will hold it in place. For flush-mount situations, align the pilaster with the guideline you made and mark the location of the screw holes. Now, drill pilot holes for the screws.

4 Finish this part of the job by repositioning the pilasters and driving screws to secure them. Just snug the screws down; you don't want to strip any threads.

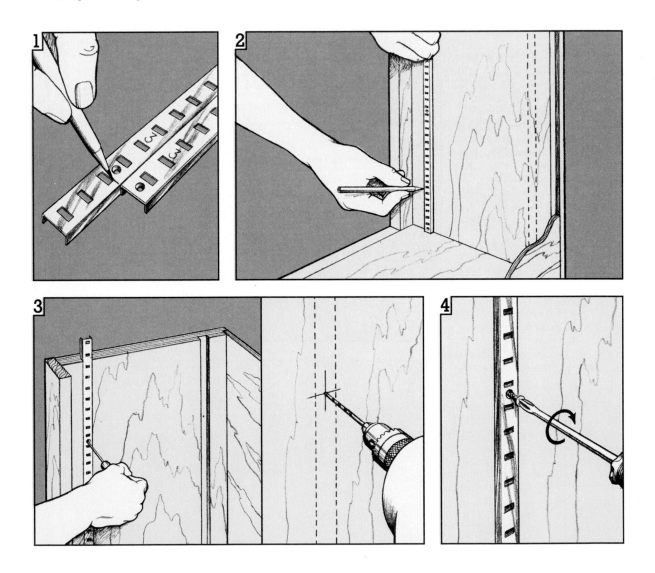

Drilling Holes for Shelf Clips or Dowels

1 Start by determining where to locate the holes. Generally, they should be positioned about one inch in from the front and back edges of the shelves. If you don't have too many holes to drill, you can first draw vertical lines to indicate the vertical center of each row of holes. Then, using a square, mark the horizontal center of each hole as shown. Finish by drilling each hole as shown.

  Notice the piece of electrical tape wrapped around the drill bit; it allows you to drill all of the holes to a uniform depth. (See sketches 2 and 3 for an easy way to accomplish the same thing.)

2 Here's a nifty solution when you're faced with having to drill a large number of holes for a cabinet or shelving unit. First, cut a piece of perforated hardboard—the type with ¼-inch-diameter holes—the same width as that of the side members and almost as high. Position it as shown and use it as a guide to cut the holes. (To avoid mix-ups, mark the top of the guide.) Here again, you'll want the holes positioned about one inch in from the front and back edges of the shelves. Electrical tape wrapped around the drill bit helps you gauge hole depth.

  Once you have finished boring all the holes in one side, simply move the template to the other side of the cabinet and bore through the same holes as before. (Be sure to keep the template in the same position when you move it; otherwise, the holes won't line up correctly.)

3 If your cabinet or shelving unit has one or more vertical dividers, your procedure is similar to that shown in sketch 2, with one important exception. When you drill holes in a divider, you must offset the holes as shown to keep from boring all the way through it.

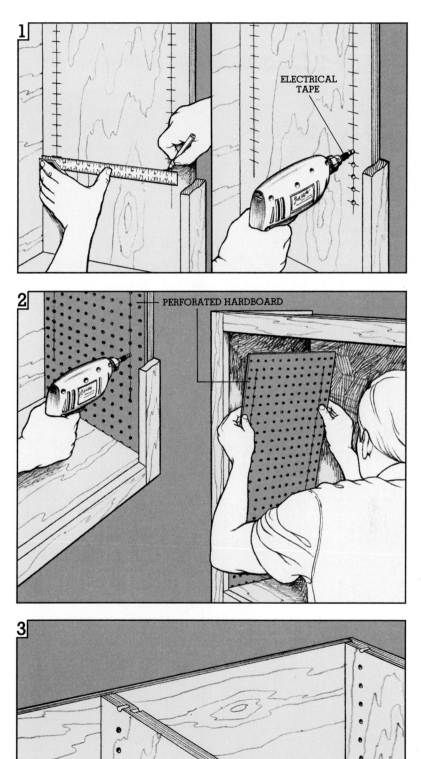

Adding Hinged Doors to Cabinets

Most hinge manufacturers assume that the consumer knows how to install their hinges, so they don't include instructions in the package. Usually, the package contains only a *pair* of hinges and enough screws to fasten the hinges in place.

What we try to do on pages 44-48 is fill a void we think exists by explaining how to install several different types of hinges, pulls, and catches.

Lipped Doors

Offset Hinges

With the door facedown, measure in an equal distance from its top and bottom and make a mark (A).

Align the hinges with your marks as shown (B), mark the location of the screws, drill pilot holes, and secure the hinges with the screws.

Now center the door over the opening, mark for and drill pilot holes (C), then hang the doors. (With lipped doors, offset hinges are your only alternative.)

Flush Doors

Butt, Decorative, and Inset Hinges

Start by measuring in an equal distance from the top and bottom of the door (usually the width of the hinge). Then, position the hinge, mark for and drill pilot holes, and fasten the hinges to the doors (A).

Center the door in the opening and rest it on a couple of nails to effect equal spacing at top and bottom. (You may have to recess one of the hinge leaves to get equal side-to-side spacing.) Mark the top and bottom of the hinge as shown (B). (With decorative hinges, just mark the location of the screw holes.)

Remove the door, chisel out a recess if necessary (C), align the hinge with the marks, and mark for and drill pilot holes in the stile (D).

Finish by hanging the door.

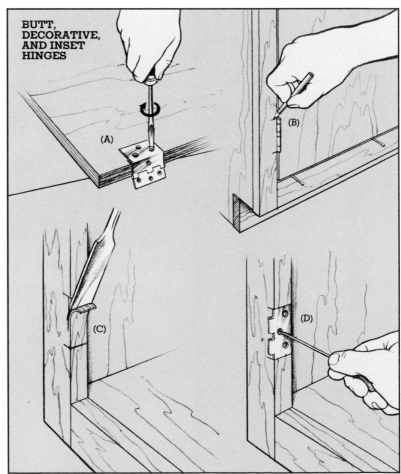

Invisible Hinges

Measure in an equal distance from the top and bottom of the door (usually the width of the hinge's leaves or about two inches) and make light marks on the face and edge of the door as shown at right (A).

Now, center the door in the opening, using nails to achieve equal top-to-bottom spacing (B). Make a corresponding mark on the stile. Be accurate; even small errors can cause big positioning problems.

Position the template as shown on both the door and stile and, using an awl, mark the drill holes (C).

Next, drill holes deep enough to accept the hinge leaves (D). Chisel out any wood left by the drilling.

Finally, drill pilot holes for the screws and mount the hinge to the door and then to the stile (E).

Concealed Hinges

(Before installing this type of hinge, mount it on scrap to avoid positioning errors. Also ask your supplier to see the manufacturer's catalog for installation particulars.)

With the door facedown, measure in two inches from its top and bottom and make light pencil marks as shown (A). Then, using a square, extend the lines out onto the back side of the door (about 2 inches).

Now, make a template as a guide for cutting the recess for the hinge's cup. (You'll be cutting the recess with a router fitted with a guide bushing.) To do this bore a hole the diameter of the cup—plus the thickness of the bushing—in a piece of wood with a spade bit or hole saw. Position the template so it is the exact distance in from the edge of the door as specified in the manufacturer's catalog and is centered over your guide mark (B). Now rout out the material to the correct depth.

Next, make a mark on the cabinet shell at the same distance from the top and bottom as for the hinge (plus clearance) (C), then fasten the hinge to its baseplate and mark the baseplate position as shown (D).

Fasten the baseplate to the cabinet and the hinge to the door (E), then mount and adjust the door to fit the opening.

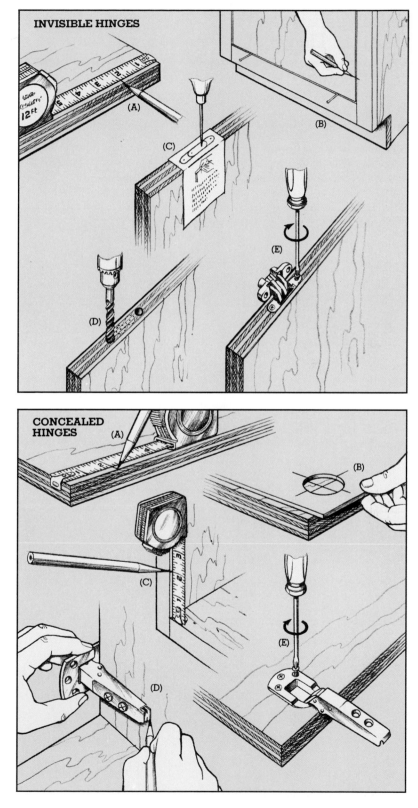

Adding Hinges to Cabinet Doors *(cont.)*

Overlay Doors

Inset and Self-Closing Hinges

With the door facedown, measure in about two inches from its top and bottom and make guide marks. Then, fasten the hinges to the doors with the screws provided (A).

Now, position the door as it will be when hung and make guide marks on the stile (B). (For overlay-with-reveal doors, first make guide marks as shown in the detail to ensure the correct reveal at each side and at top and bottom.)

Carefully align the hinges with the guide marks on the stile, mark the location of the screw holes (C), drill pilot holes, and secure the door to the frame, adjusting the hinges as necessary for a good fit.

Pivot Hinges

Start by making a pair of cuts the thickness of the hinge leaf on the hinge side of the doors with a table saw (A). Practice on scrap first to avoid cutting mistakes.

Secure the hinges to the door with screws (B), then position the door against the face frame and mark the location of the hinges on the stile (C). Finish the installation by mounting the door to the face frame (D) and adjusting, if necessary.

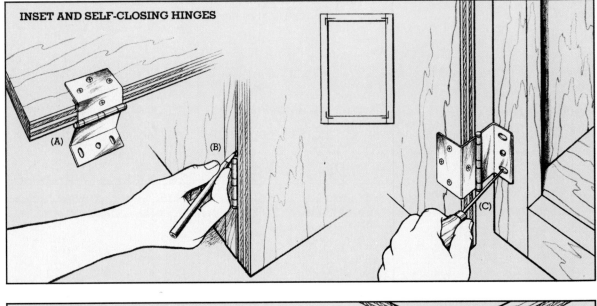

INSET AND SELF-CLOSING HINGES

(A) (B) (C)

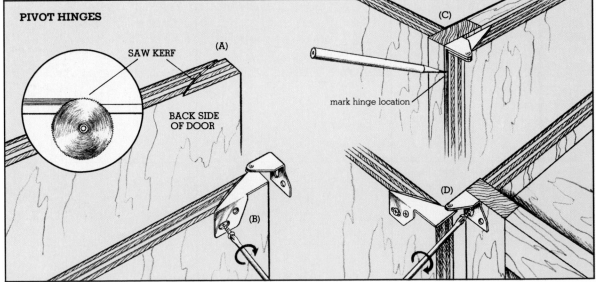

PIVOT HINGES

SAW KERF (A)

BACK SIDE OF DOOR

(B)

(C)

mark hinge location

(D)

Concealed Hinges

(When you purchase this type of hinge, ask your supplier to show you the manufacturer's catalog describing your hinge; it contains essential mounting information you can't get elsewhere. Also, to avoid positioning errors, mount the hinge on scrap before installing it on the door itself.)

Measure in an equal distance from the top and bottom of the door (usually about two inches) and mark the location of the hinges as shown at right. Extend the marks on the back side of the door about two inches (A).

Make a template as described on page 45 under "concealed hinges" and cut the hinge cup recesses to the correct depth (B).

Fasten the hinges to the door with screws (C) and position the door against the face frame. Mark the location of the hinges on the stile (D), then with the door opened, fasten the hinges to the stile (E); adjust if needed.

Glass and Plastic Doors

Flush Glass Doors

To mount the hinge shown at right, drill a pair of holes near the edge of the top rail and one near the edge of the bottom one (make them deep enough to accept the sleeves and bullet catch).

Then, fit the sleeves and catch into the holes and tap them into place with a hammer and block of scrap wood.

Slip the hinges into the sleeves, fit the doors into the hinges' channels, adjust the doors so they clear the face frame, and tighten the holding screws on the hinges.

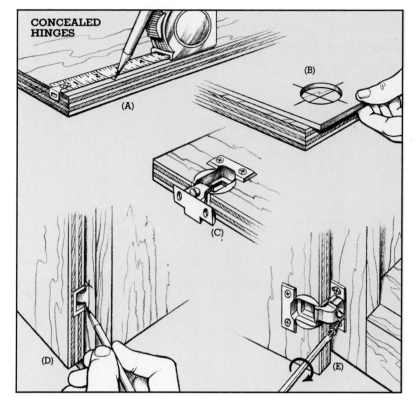

CONCEALED HINGES

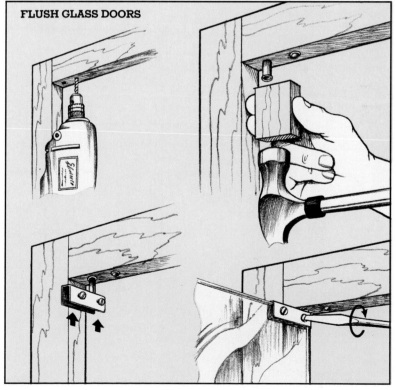

FLUSH GLASS DOORS

Adding Hinges to Cabinet Doors *(cont.)*

Overlay Glass Doors

(When purchasing this type of hinge, have your supplier show you the mounting instructions in the product catalog; it contains information you need to install the hinge. Also, it's best to have the holes in the doors cut professionally.)

Start by positioning each door as it will be when hung and make marks on the cabinet that align with the horizontal center of the holes in the door (A). Now, fasten the hinges to the baseplates, align the hinges with the guide marks, and mark the location of the baseplates (B).

Fasten the baseplates to the cabinet and the hinges to the door with screws. Connect the hinges to the baseplates and adjust the door (C).

Installing Catches and Pulls

Fastening these hardware items to cabinets isn't difficult, but there are a few general rules you need to be aware of before beginning. First, you should locate the catch as close as possible to the handle or pull to avoid undue pressure on the hardware. Second, the latch portion of the catch mounts on the cabinet; the strike, on the door. And third, the position of the pull itself is determined by the position of the cabinet it's being installed on. Typically, with base cabinets, you'll find them near the top of the door; with upper cabinets, near the bottom.

1 To mount typical pulls, drill the required number of holes where desired, position the pull, and secure with screws. (Fit the continuous pulls, as shown, onto the door and screw in place. Trim the door first to allow for the pull's thickness.)

2 Mount catches by screwing the latch to the cabinet, then positioning the strike and securing it to the door.

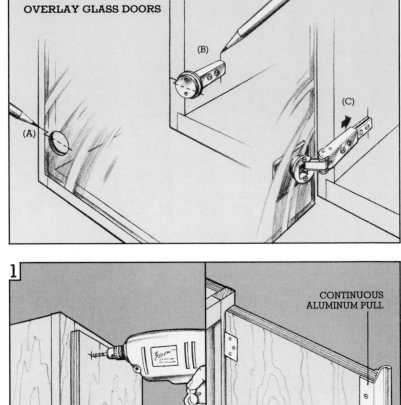

OVERLAY GLASS DOORS

(A)   (B)   (C)

CONTINUOUS ALUMINUM PULL

1

2

press door against strike to mark

STILE

SHARP MARKING POINTS

VIEW FROM BELOW

Adding Sliding Doors to Cabinets

1 Start by cutting the doors to the size specified in your plan (see page 30). Then, if you're using aluminum or plastic track, cut two lengths of it and screw them to the cabinet's top and bottom panels. Remember, the track with the deeper channels goes on top; the shallower channels, at the bottom. If your cabinet has a face frame, fit the track against its back side. If not, position it about ¼ inch in from the cabinet's front edge. (On cabinets with face frames, you'll need to put a spacer block above the top track so the track's bottom edge will be flush with the bottom of the face frame.)

If you've opted for a vinyl spline-type track, you will have already cut the grooves for the splines, so just press them into the recesses. If you find the going tough, tap them gently with a hammer.

2 Now, if you're dealing with thin doors, bore a hole through each door. These serve as your pulls. For thicker doors, drill holes partway through the material (see the package directions for correct size and depth of the holes). Locate the holes about ¾ inch in from the outside edge of the doors and center them vertically. Then, friction-fit the pulls into their holes.

Lastly, fit the door panels—the rear one first, the front one last—into their channels, top edge first. Lift up on them until the bottom edge clears the lower track. They should then drop into the channel.

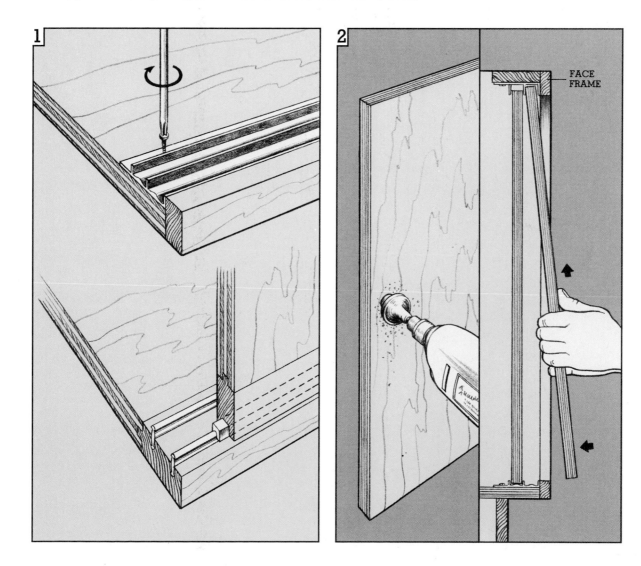

FACE FRAME

Adding Drawers to Cabinets

In the planning section, we showed you how to fit a cabinet's drawers together (see pages 27-29). The emphasis here, however, is on correctly positioning the drawer in the opening. We'll show two ways to do this—side-mounted metal slides and side-mounted wooden ones.

Before installing the metal type, be sure to read the directions that accompany the slide. They all mount somewhat differently. Also, if your unit has flush drawers, you'll have to put a piece of scrap at the back of the cabinet to stop the drawers flush with the front of the face frame.

Side-Mount Metal Slides

1 If you're installing this type of metal slide, position the drawer part of the slide so that the front of it butts against the back side of the drawer front, and the flange on the other end aligns with the bottom of the side of the drawer. Secure the flanged end with a screw. Now, move the front of the slide up or down so the slide is parallel to the drawer side. Drive a screw in the hole provided to secure it. Finish screwing the slide to the side. Repeat this for the other slide.

2 To install the mating part of the metal slide, position it as shown, with a piece of plastic laminate below the slide to provide clearance. If you're installing a bank of drawers without rails between them, lay plastic laminate on the top edge of the drawer below the one you're installing. (In most instances, you'll first need to nail a filler strip to the cabinet side to serve as a nailing surface for the drawer slide.)

Now, secure the slide's front end by driving a screw into the face frame. Using a torpedo level, level the slide's other end and secure it with screws.

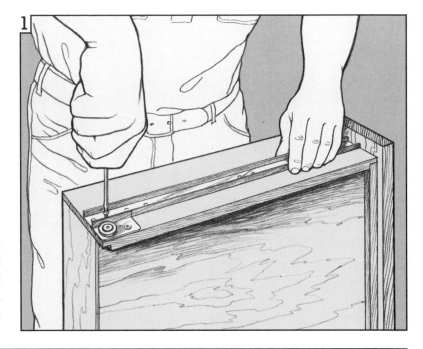

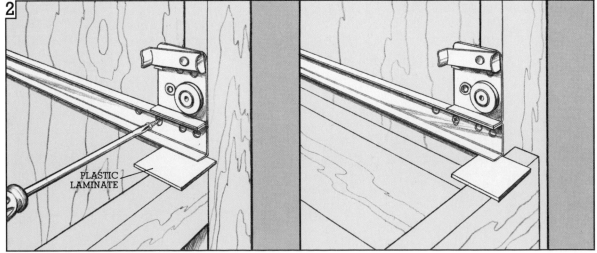

PLASTIC LAMINATE

Side-Mount Wooden Slides

1 First, mark the location of the two cleats you'll be attaching to each side. Center them vertically, and so that they are parallel with the drawer, being sure to allow enough room between them to accept the cleat that will be nailed to the cabinet. Run a bead of glue along each mark, then position and nail the cleats with brads or small finishing nails.

2 Now, fit the drawer into the opening and place a nail near each edge of the drawer, as shown, to provide clearance. Using a pencil, mark the location of the cleats you will be attaching to the cabinet. (If you're dealing with a bank of drawers not separated by face frames, set the nails on top of the drawer beneath the one you're installing.)

Using a framing square, extend the guide marks, then using glue and brads or small finishing nails, secure the cleats.

Attaching False Fronts to Cabinets

In some cabinet situations, when you need to hide a plumbing fixture from view, you'll want to install a false front, which is nothing more than a door or drawer look-alike that doesn't open or pull out. The instructions below and the sketch at right show you how to do this.

Cut the false front to the size specified in your plan. Then, cut a couple of scrap blocks and drill a pilot hole near each end of each one. Secure the blocks to the back side of the face frame as shown with glue and screws, then position the front and drive screws through the blocks into the front's back side.

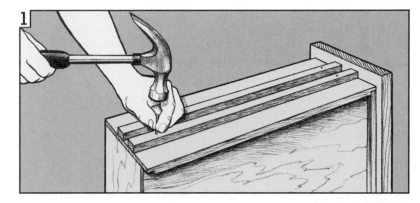

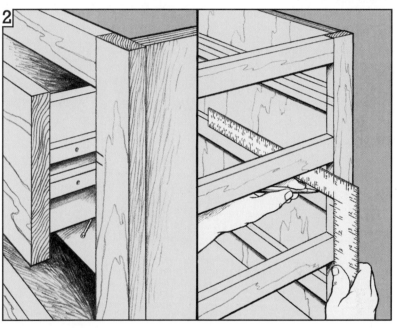

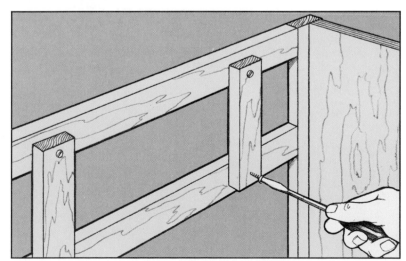

Applying a Finish to the Cabinet

Cabinetmakers know that no matter how well built a cabinetry project is, no amount of woodworking expertise can make up for a lousy finish. In fact, many pros insist that the customer do the finishing to avoid hassles over this important part of the project. So whatever you do, take the time to do this job right.

Basically, there are two fin-ishing procedures—painting or clear finishing—and on these two pages, we explain a method for using each.

When using any finishing product, read the label to be sure that you know what the manufacturer says about use and application.

If you're covering the cabinet with plastic laminate, see pages 55-57 for applying.

Painting

1 If you haven't already recessed all nails with a nail set and hammer, do so now. Then, do any necessary sanding with 150-grit sandpaper. Remove all dust with a tack cloth.

Now, using a primer that's compatible with the finish you choose, apply a prime coat to all surfaces. Allow the paint to dry.

2 Lightly sand the unit again, then inspect the surfaces for imperfections and unfilled nail holes. Fill these with spackling compound, let the compound dry, and sand it smooth.

3 Reprime the filled surfaces, let the primer dry, spot-sand these areas, wipe the entire unit with a tack cloth to remove any remaining dust, and apply the finish coat. (You may want to apply several coats of paint to build up the surface. If so, lightly sand the surface between coats.)

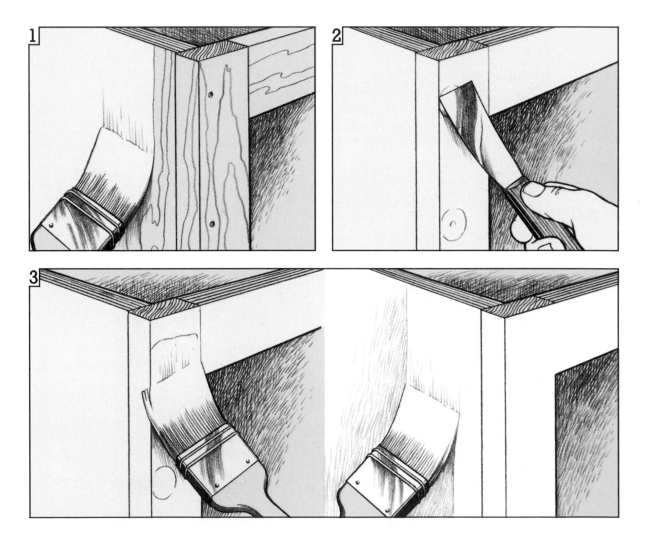

Clear Finishing

1 Start by sanding the surfaces smooth with 150-grit sandpaper and wiping off the dust with a tack cloth. If your project is made with an open-grain wood such as oak, mahogany, or walnut, use a wood filler to close the pores prior to staining, if desired. This helps to tame the pronounced grain of these woods. (Some products on the market fill, stain, and seal at the same time.)

To apply filler, use a clean, dry brush to work the filler into the surface from all directions. After 10 to 15 minutes, level the filler by dragging a piece of cardboard across the wood grain. Finally, when the filler is almost dry, carefully drag the surface again—this time with the wood grain.

If you decide not to use filler on your project, go ahead and stain the wood, using a brush or a clean stain-saturated rag. (Before deciding, you may want to test a wood scrap using both methods to see what effect you get.) After waiting the amount of time specified on the container label, wipe off the excess stain with a clean rag. Allow the stain to dry.

2 Unless you used a sealer stain, in which event you can skip this step, now apply a sanding sealer to seal in the stain. Using a clean, dry brush, work the sealer into the wood from several directions, but always finish brushing with the grain, using long, even strokes.

After the sealer dries completely, sand with the grain, using a sanding block. (You can also hand-sand without the block.) Don't worry when the wood takes on a whitish color. Clean the surface with a tack cloth to remove the residue.

3 Next, fill all nail holes and other imperfections with wood putty. (You may have to experiment to get a good color match.) And finally, apply one or more coats of finish. At right, we show tung oil being rubbed onto the surface, but some people prefer the look of polyurethane or other finishes. See the label directions for application advice.

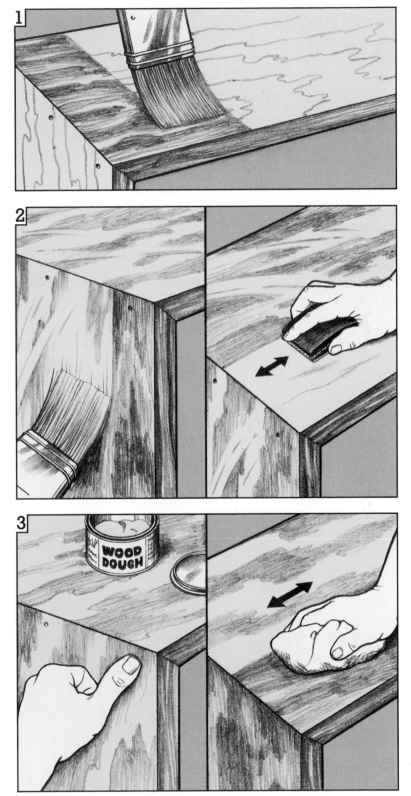

Installing Cabinets

A neat-looking cabinet installation requires that you hang
or position your unit so it is
plumb and level. But that's not
the only prerequisite. You also
must be concerned with securing it adequately to the wall
and floor or ceiling. In the
illustrations below, we show
you how to achieve both of
these marks of good cabinetry.
(Since custom cabinets—
especially banks of them—
weigh plenty, you'll need an
assistant or two for this part of
the project.)

1 Start by marking the outline of the
unit(s) on the floor and walls, using a
framing square and a chalk line. Doing this allows you to spot potential
positioning problems prior to the actual installation. Also locate the wall
studs that run behind the cabinet(s)
and mark their location with a chalk
line. Extend the lines far enough that
you can still see them when the cabinets are raised into place.

2 Now, move the cabinet(s) into the
desired position. If you're installing
a bank of cabinets similar to the situation shown in sketch 1, start with
the upper cabinets first, and work
from the corner outward. If yours
are wall-hung cabinets, it helps to
nail a ledger strip to the wall along
the line defining the bottom of the
cabinets before hoisting them up.

Again, if you are hanging wall-
hung units, you'll find it easier to
make the face frames of adjoining
cabinets flush with each other if you
join as many cabinets as you can
manage before positioning them.
To do this, lay the units on their back
and clamp their face frames together. Then drill pilot holes
through the edges of the face frame
members, and screw them together.

3 Have your assistant check the
cabinets for plumb and level while
you shim as necessary.

4 Drill pilot holes through the ledg-
er(s) and into the studs, then drive
good-size screws to secure the unit
to the wall. To provide even more
stability, screw or nail the unit to the
floor or ceiling (or bulkhead).

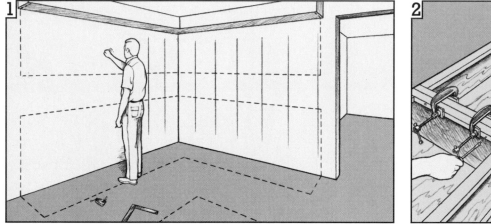

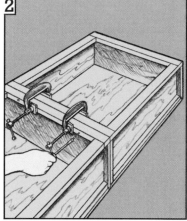

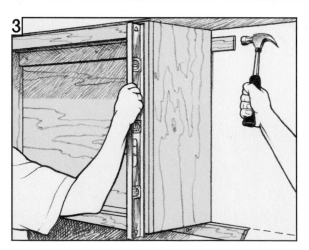

Installing Counter Tops

Today, you have several counter-top options (see pages 12-13), and with most, the installation procedures vary only slightly. With site-built counter tops, you first build the top, then fasten it to the cabinet. If your plans include plastic laminate as the surface material, apply it at the same time you're building the top. Ceramic tiles and other such materials go on after the top has been fastened to the cabinet. (See pages 60-61 for more on ceramic tile installation.)

For all other types, though, the finish material is in place when you purchase the top, so all that remains is to fasten it to the cabinet. On pages 55-61, we take you step by step through each option.

Site-Built Tops

1 Cut a piece of ¾-inch particleboard or plywood to the size specified in your plan. (If one end of your cabinet fits up against a wall, as the one shown here does, the top should overlap the other end and the front by one inch. If both ends butt against walls, cut the top flush with both ends and overlap the front by one inch. And for cabinets whose ends don't butt against walls, allow 1-inch overlap at both ends and the front.) Test-fit the top and make adjustments to compensate for irregularities.

2 Now, turn the top upside-down and glue and nail 1x2s (or ¾-inch particleboard or plywood strips) around its perimeter as shown. (For more stability, install bracing at the top of the cabinet.)

3 (Steps 3-8 apply to plastic laminate installations. If you'll be surfacing with ceramic tile, skip down to *(continued)*

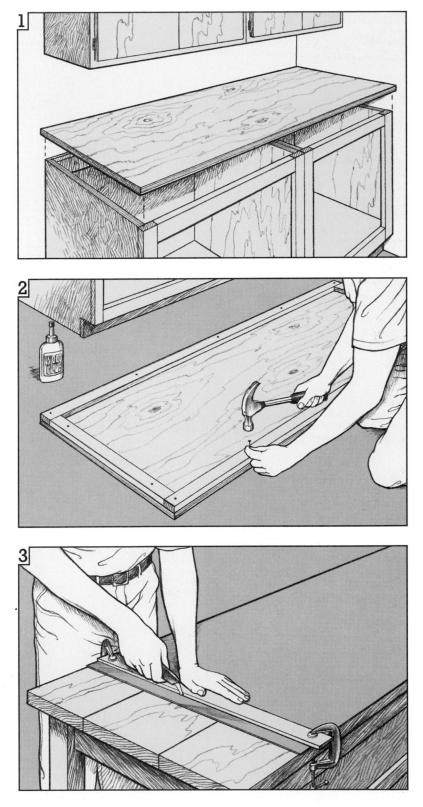

Installing
Counter Tops *(cont.)*

step 9 and see pages 60-61.) Cut the banding strips for the edges of the counter top.

You can cut plastic laminate two ways, depending on the tools you have at your disposal. Some professional installers start by measuring the size of the piece that they'll need (allowing a ½-inch overlap in all instances). Then, they lay a straight-edge along the cutoff line and score the face of the laminate with a carbide-tipped cutting tool similar to the one shown at right. To finish the cut, they snap the laminate toward the scored line.

You also can cut laminate with several types of electric saws. To do this, first score the face of the laminate with an awl or other sharp-pointed object, then saw along the scored line with a saber, circular, or table saw and a fine-toothed blade.

To make inside cuts, use a drill to make an opening large enough to enable you to insert the saw blade, then finish the cut with the saw. (To prevent plastic laminate from stress cracking, you must radius inside corners at least ¼ inch.)

4 Before adhering the banding to the top's edges (or any laminate to any surface), you must prepare the surface correctly. With new surfaces, make sure you fill all voids with wood putty, then after allowing the putty to dry, sand the entire surface smooth. With already-finished surfaces, remove paint or other finish by sanding, then repeat the procedure for new surfaces.

Now, apply contact cement to both the core material and the back side of the laminate, allow the cement to dry, then *carefully* position the laminate so it overlaps the top. and bottom of the edge. To ensure maximum adhesion of the contact cement, use a hammer and wood block or a rubber mallet to make sure the cemented surfaces meet. Sand the excess laminate with a belt sander, being careful not to burn it.

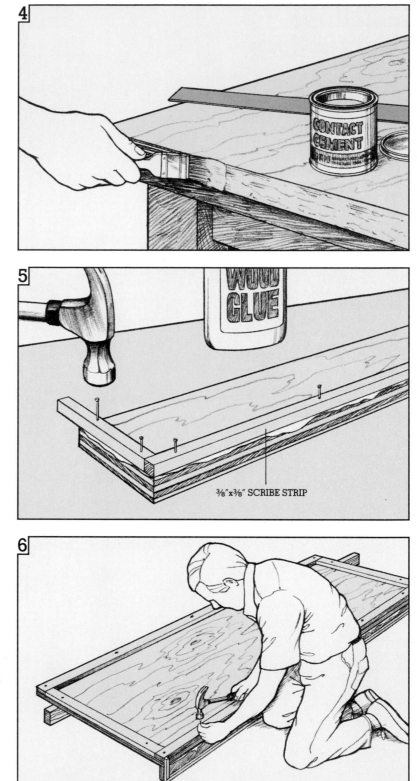

³⁄₈" x ³⁄₈" SCRIBE STRIP

5 If you plan to have a laminated backsplash and/or endsplashes, cut a 4-inch-wide piece of ¾-inch particleboard or plywood to the length needed. With glue and brads driven partway in, attach a ⅜x⅜-inch *scribe strip* flush with the top edge of the splash. (Brads should be pulled out later.) Now, cover the face of the splash with laminate and sand off the excess as described in step 4. Then, laminate the top edge of the splash (and the ends, if applicable), and trim the back but not the front edge.

6 Run a bead of glue along the bottom edge of the splash, let the glue get tacky, position the splash on the counter top, and nail the two together as shown on page 56.

7 Cut the counter-top laminate to the size needed (be sure to allow excess on all sides) and apply contact cement to the back side of the laminate and the counter-top surface. Allow the cement to dry. Now, lay kraft or waxed paper on the counter surface, position the laminate, and remove the paper gradually. Tap the surface with a hammer and wooden block or a rubber mallet to ensure a good bond.

8 After tapping the laminate, begin trimming the excess. If you have a router, use it and a laminate-cutting bit. If not, you can get satisfactory results with a double-cut hand file. A 7-degree bevel is standard. If you're using a router, be sure to keep it moving as you work. Otherwise, you'll burn the surface.

9 Lift the counter top onto the cabinet and check it for a good fit. If you see gaps between the top and the wall, use a compass or a pencil to follow the contour of the wall. Trim away excess with a block plane. Recheck the fit, then run a bead of glue around the top edge of the cabinet. Position the top, and from underneath, secure it to the cabinet with corner braces. (If you plan to set a sink or lavatory into the counter top, position the fixture template, then make the cutout with a saber saw.)

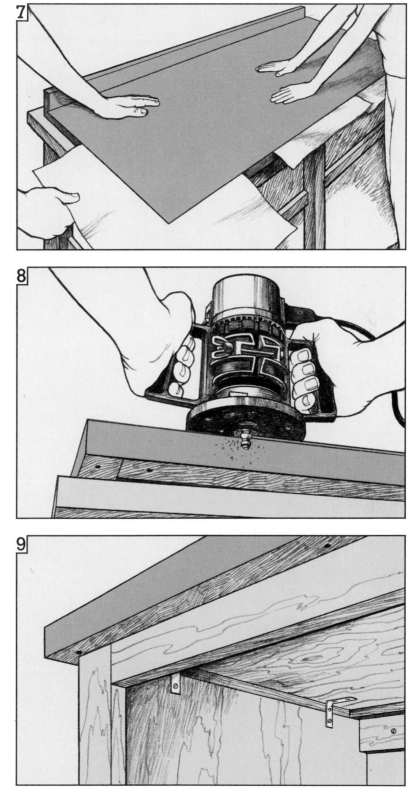

Installing Counter Tops *(cont.)*

Post-Formed Tops

1 Start by setting the top on the cabinet. It should overlap the cabinet uniformly at the front. If it doesn't or if you can see gaps between the counter top and the wall it butts against, lay a pencil up against the wall and make a scribe line. Then, using a saber saw, block plane, or a coping saw, cut along the line. (If you're installing a two-piece top, you'll have to make sure the pieces fit together at the correct angle and that they rest flush against the wall.)

2 To join a two-piece post-formed counter top, set both pieces onto the cabinet (after you have test-fit them). Then, apply a bead of glue to one of the mating surfaces, and from underneath, partially tighten the bolts or other connecting devices that came with the product. Now, check the surface of the counter at the joint line. Both pieces should be on the same plane. If one is higher than the other, use a hammer and wooden block to move them into alignment. When you're satisfied, tighten down the bolts.

3 There are a couple of ways to secure a post-formed top to cabinets. If you used wood bracing for additional support of the top, you can drive screws through the bracing and into the counter top's underside. Or you can make the connection with metal corner braces.

To fasten a counter top to an unreinforced cabinet, screw metal corner braces to the ledger at the rear of the cabinet and to the back side of the face frame as well as to the counter top. Three or four braces at the front and back will normally be sufficient.

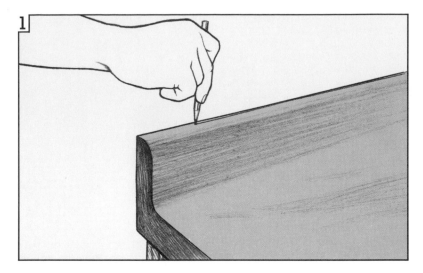

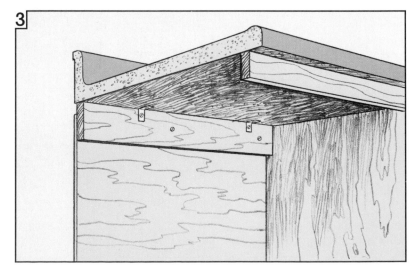

Cultured and Natural Marble Tops

1 Both of these products are ready to install right out of their package. And you install both in exactly the same way. Start by test-fitting the top. It should extend about one inch beyond the front edge of the cabinet and one inch beyond the cabinet sides if they're exposed. (Top should be flush if sides are not exposed.) If the fit isn't correct, cut the cultured tops to fit along the edge that won't show; with natural marble, it's best to have your supplier recut it.

Run a bead of panel adhesive along the top edge of the cabinet and allow it to set up briefly.

2 Lift the counter into position and weight it down with some heavy objects. Finish the project by installing the sink or lavatory and/or faucets.

High-Density Plastic Tops

1A First glue and nail 1x2s to the top edge of the cabinet. Then position the top. (It should extend one inch beyond the front and all exposed sides. Also, allow ⅛ inch between the counter and walls.) Make any needed cuts with a circular saw. Mark the location of any cutouts, such as for a sink. With the top adequately supported, partially cut the opening with a router; allow a ⅜-inch radius at the corners.

2A Now, carefully move the top into position, finish cutting the opening, then have an assistant lift up the top while you apply panel adhesive to the 1x2s as shown.

If you're joining two sections together, position them ½ inch apart on the cabinet, lay a ¼-inch bead of silicone caulk between them, and then slide the sections together to form a tight joint.

Press the top into place and weight it with some heavy objects. Round off the corners with fine sandpaper. Trim the front edge, if desired, by applying a 1-inch-wide strip of the same material. Then, glue the backsplash to the wall.

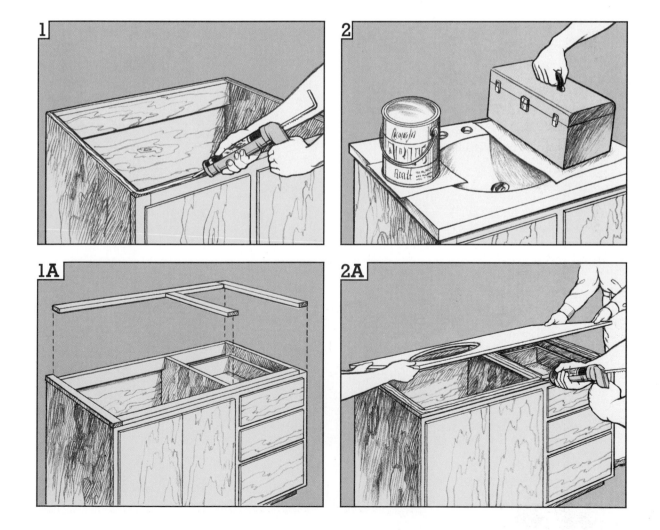

Surfacing Counter Tops with Ceramic Tile

Of all of your counter-top options, ceramic tile is unquestionably the most long-lasting and maintenance-free. And, as we explain below, installing it doesn't necessarily require the services of a professional tile setter.

Ceramic tile adapts to a variety of surfaces including plywood and particleboard. Too, it adapts to existing surfaces such as plastic laminate, wood, and tiled tops. The sketches and instructions on these two pages describe the thin-set method of tile installation.

1 If your counter top already is covered, rough up the surface with coarse abrasive. If not, start by laying out the tiles as shown, allowing space between each for grout. Note how the procedure differs depending on whether you have a one-piece straight top or a two-piece (or more) version. Other factors affecting placement are the way you finish off the front edge of the counter top and how the back row is handled. Regardless of which way you choose, though, chances are you'll need to adjust the position of the tiles or the spacing between tiles to achieve a pleasing effect. Generally, it's best to have full tiles at the front edge of the counter top and save any necessary cutting for the tiles at the rear. If the ends of the counter top abut walls, or if neither does, center the tiles side to side. If one end does and the other doesn't, you'll want the full tiles at the open end. When you're satisfied with the position of the tiles, mark the corners of the starter tile with brads, then remove the tiles.

2 Using the mortar (adhesive) recommended by your tile dealer, spread a $^3/_{32}$-inch layer of it over a 3-foot-square area with a square-notched trowel. Then place the first tile, with a slight twisting motion. Tap it gently with a rubber mallet

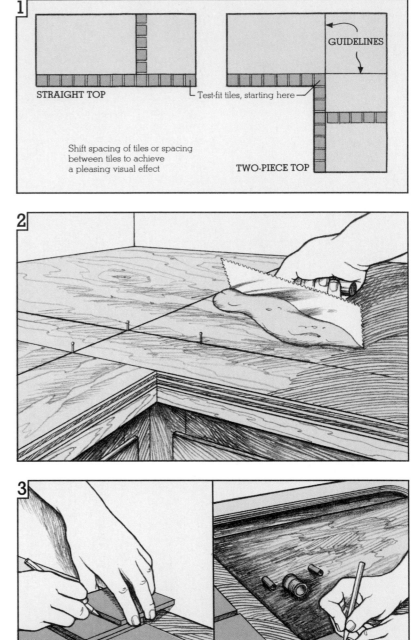

1 STRAIGHT TOP

GUIDELINES

Test-fit tiles, starting here

TWO-PIECE TOP

Shift spacing of tiles or spacing between tiles to achieve a pleasing visual effect

2

3

and a fabric-covered wooden block to ensure good adhesion. Repeat this procedure until you have set all of the full tiles.

3 Once the full tiles are in place, measure and cut the border tiles. To do this, set another full tile on top of one in the back or end row, set another on top of the second (but against the wall or outer edge of the counter top), and mark the middle tile as shown. Don't forget to include any joint spacing in your calculations. Measure for each tile, as the wall may not be square, then cut the border tiles with a tile cutter or a saw fitted with an abrasive blade. If you have just a few tiles to cut, you can also score the surface of the tiles with a glass cutter, then snap them back with your hand.

To fit tiles around the perimeter of a sink or other opening, position a full tile as shown and mark the cut line. Cut these with an abrasive blade.

4 To finish off the edges of the counter top with tile, first measure and cut the tiles. Then, spread adhesive onto the back of each tile and press into place.

Now, set the backsplash tiles, making sure that they align with those on the counter top.

5 After letting the adhesive set up for the time specified on the adhesive container, apply grout to the surface with a rubber-faced trowel. Apply firm, downward pressure, and move the trowel in one direction to prevent air from being trapped in the joints.

6 Allow the grout to set up somewhat (check label directions). Then, clean the excess from the tiles with a sponge. Be patient here, as you'll have to make numerous passes. Rinse the sponge with clean water as needed.

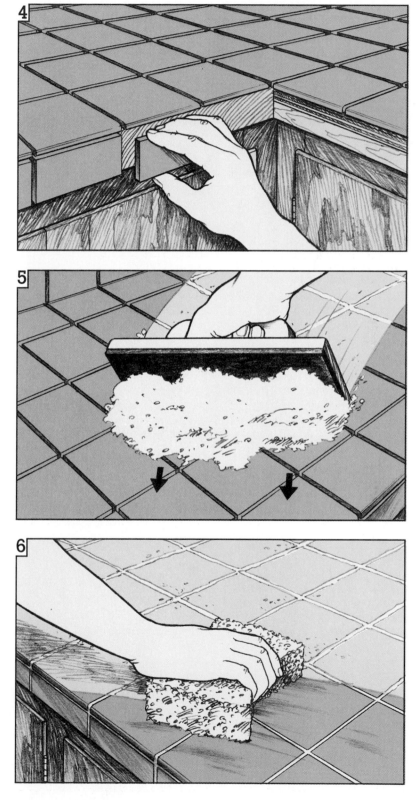

CUTTING AND JOINING TECHNIQUES

Fashioning wood to exact dimensions and joining it with precision require more than just a steady hand and 20/20 vision. You also must possess a working knowledge of some techniques used by cabinetmakers. This chapter will familiarize you with some of those techniques. In it we show you how to make crosscuts, rips, angle and bevel cuts, dadoes, grooves, and rabbets as well as several reliable ways to join wood. We avoid, however, some of the more difficult and time-consuming joinery such as dovetail and mortise and tenon joints. With today's strong glues, they're simply not necessary.

You'll notice, too, that we include safety reminders in red type. Because the power tools we show—portable circular saw, table saw, and router—can be dangerous if used improperly, read and obey these cautions, as well as the following safety and operating tips:

• Keep your work area clean and dry, and avoid dressing in loose-fitting clothes or wearing jewelry that could catch in a power tool's moving parts.
• Wear goggles while operating a power tool and check to see if all safety mechanisms are properly installed.
• Read and obey safety rules and tool use information in owner's manuals.
• Maintain sharp bits and blades.
• Never change or adjust a blade or bit without first unplugging the tool.
• Don't plug in a power tool until you've checked its cord and plug for defects.
• Secure your workpiece before cutting.
• Measure twice.
• Test cuts on scrap before working on the real thing.
• To prevent splintering, provide adequate support for the scrap side of the workpiece.
• Let the tool reach full power before using it.

Making the Basic Cuts

Making Cuts with A Circular Saw

Many people think that building a cabinet or shelving unit first requires a major investment in tools. Not so! Though not the ideal tool for making cabinets and shelving units, a portable circular saw will perform well if you're patient and have a good straightedge.

When using a circular saw, keep these points in mind:
• Always stand to one side of the work to avoid serious injury from kickback.
• Raise the guard when first making a cut so it doesn't catch on the workpiece edge.
• For best looks, face the good side of the workpiece down when cutting.
• Keep plenty of slack in the cord so it doesn't hang up.
• Prevent binding and ensure a straight cut by using a guide.
• If the saw should bind, release the switch immediately.

Crosscutting

1 To check a blade set perpendicular to the base, unplug the saw and use a combination square as shown here; to check lesser angles, go with a T-bevel. If you need to adjust the angle, loosen the wing nut on the bevel scale and turn the base to the desired angle. Then tighten the nut.

Now is also the time to check and, if necessary, adjust the blade depth. To do this, rest the saw on the edge of the work and loosen the appropriate locking mechanism. Raise or lower the base until the blade extends below the workpiece by ⅛ to ¼ inch. Tighten the wing nut.

2 To determine how far to clamp your straightedge guide from the in-

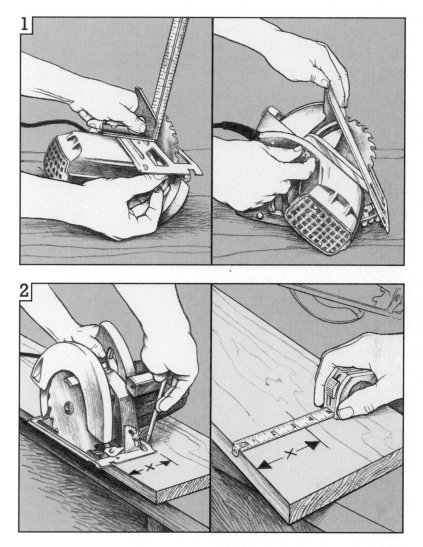

tended cutoff line, hold the saw against the workpiece edge as shown above and mark the location of the edge of the saw base. Next, measure the distance between the workpiece edge and the mark. This distance varies depending on the blade you use.

3 To make the cut, position the saw firmly against the straightedge, then enter the work. To prevent the wood from splintering, have a helper support the scrap end of the work.

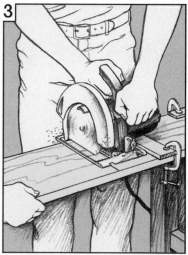

Rip Cutting

If you're making a cut more than 6 inches from the lumber's edge, as shown below, make your cut line marks at each end of the material, snap a chalk line between them, then clamp a straightedge the appropriate distance from the cut line. (See sketches 1 and 2 on page 63 for setting up your saw and straightedge.) To allow room for the blade underneath, support the sheet using four 2x4s.

If your cut line measures less than 6 inches from the edge, attach a rip guide to your saw. Adjust it according to the width of the cut desired, then begin sawing, keeping the rip guide flush to the workpiece edge. **NOTE: To prevent the blade from binding, stop the saw in the middle of the cut and place a nail or thin wooden wedge into the existing kerf.**

Angle Cutting

1 To strike a 45-degree cut line on a piece of wood, position a combination square as shown in sketch 1. On large pieces of material, such as sheets, continue the cut line out using an aligned straightedge. For angles other than 45 or 90 degrees, use a T-bevel.

2 Now position the straightedge the correct distance from the cut line and clamp it and the workpiece down. (See sketches 1 and 2 on page 63 for setting up your saw and straightedge.) Rest the front of the saw base on the work and against the angled straightedge, allow the blade to come to full speed, then begin your cut.

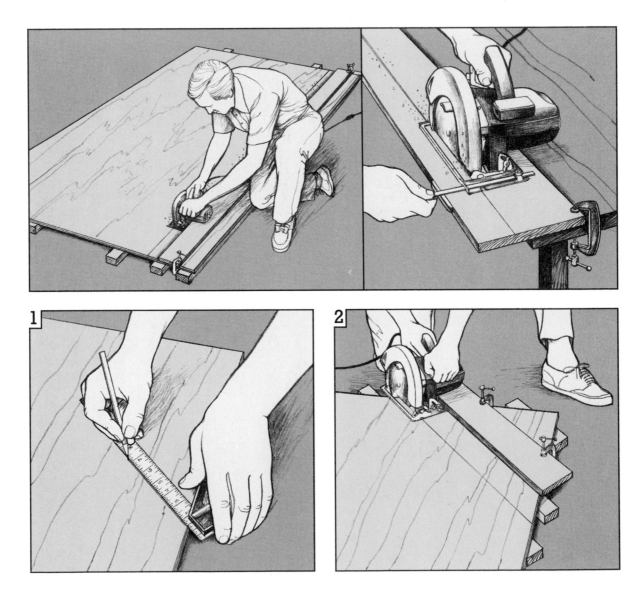

Beveling

1 If you know the exact bevel angle in degrees, turn your circular saw upside down and loosen the locking nut along the bevel scale. Note that on most saws this scale ranges from 0 to 45 degrees. **WARNING: Before making any adjustment, un-plug the saw.** Now tilt the base until the guide mark aligns with the correct increment along the scale and tighten the wing nut.

If you don't know the exact angle, use a T-bevel to obtain it. Then resting this tool between the saw base and blade, tilt the base until the base/blade angle matches that of the T-bevel. Complete the adjustment by turning the appropriate nut and locking the saw base.

2 Because the distance between the saw blade and saw base edge changes when you tilt the blade for a bevel cut, a new measurement must be taken for placing your straightedge (see sketch 2, page 63). You'll probably have to adjust the blade depth, too, so it's ⅛ to ¼ inch below the material you intend to cut (see sketch 1, page 63). **NOTE: Make a test cut on scrap to determine if the angle you get is exactly what you want.**

As a final preparation before cutting, extend the surface cut line onto the edge where you'll begin the cut. This will permit you to double-check your blade alignment. Now clamp on your straightedge, plug in the saw, and place its base on the edge of the workpiece and flush to the guide. Sight along the blade to see if its angle agrees with the cut line, then depress the saw switch and begin sawing.

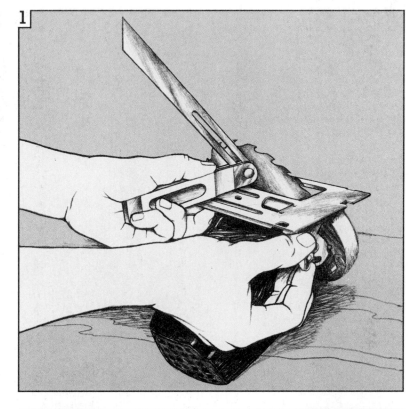

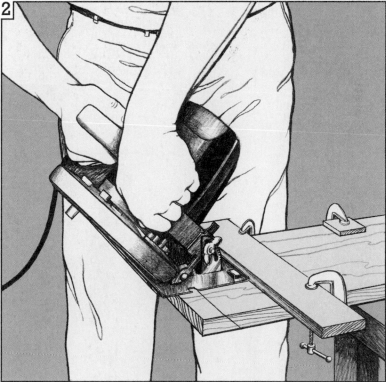

Dadoing and Grooving

Using a square, draw two parallel lines that define the borders of the channel to be cut. Clamp a straight-edge at the appropriate distance from one of the borders (see sketch 2, page 63). Keep in mind, however, that the saw kerf should run along the inside edge of the channel. Now, **with the saw unplugged,** adjust the saw blade to the desired dado depth (⅓ to ½ the thickness of the goods). Plug in the saw and begin your cut along the straightedge.

Next, move your straightedge and make a cut along the other cutting line.

Plow out the remaining material by making additional passes with the saw. Finish by removing burrs or rough spots with a chisel.

Rabbeting

Measure in from the edge of the workpiece the width of the rabbet you desire and mark the location of your cut line. Set up a straightedge (see sketch 2, page 63), keeping the kerf on the waste side of the line. Now, **with the saw unplugged,** adjust the saw blade to match the rabbet depth (see sketch 1, page 63), plug in the saw, and proceed with the cut.

Working toward the edge, free-hand the remaining number of saw passes needed to clean the rabbet out. Remove any rough spots along the rabbet with a chisel.

Note in part 2 how to rabbet narrow stock, a procedure that's a bit more involved. Here you need to frame in the workpiece with a jig made from scrap of the same thickness. This provides support for the saw base, offering you more control over the saw. Continue, following the instructions above for rabbeting wider material.

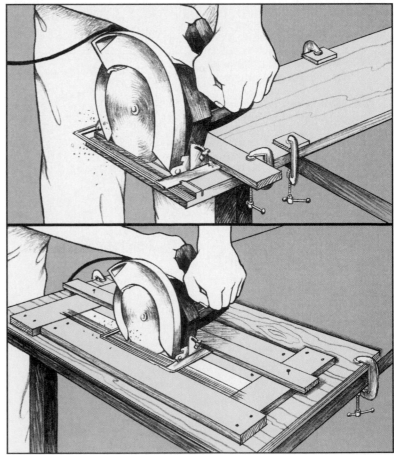

Making Cuts With a Table Saw

Measuring mistakes aside, cutting errors occur for two reasons: either the tool doing the cutting wanders from its intended path, or the workpiece moves around too much during the cut. With a table saw, such control problems are minor.

The table saw is a stationary power tool; it can't move around like the hand-held circular saw. And with the aid of the rip fence, miter gauge (standard accessories), and other aids shown below, you can feed material (good side up) into the blade, and it will come out as precisely cut as can be expected.

A table saw's other virtues include its versatility—it can make all the cuts required of the cabinetmaker—and its ease of adjustment.

Keep in mind, however, that this tool demands your utmost respect. In addition to the general safety tips covered on page 62, avoid injury by heeding the specific table saw tips listed below and in your operator's manual:
• Always stand to one side of the blade while sawing.
• Keep your fingers at least 6 inches away from the blade during the saw's operation.
• Never remove the guard apparatus unless it interferes with the cut.
• Avoid making freehand cuts; instead, use the proper guides and saw helps for each cut.

Crosscutting

1 Before making a cut, **unplug the saw** and, using a combination square, check to see if the blade is square to the table. If it isn't, turn the *tilt handwheel* (located under the table surface) and recheck for square. Then crank the *elevation handwheel* so the blade extends ⅛ inch above the workpiece.

Now adjust the miter gauge to zero and plug in the saw. With the workpiece on the table and against the miter gauge, align the cut line with the saw blade so that the kerf ends up on the scrap side of the line. Turn on the saw and slowly feed the workpiece into the blade.

When cutting long lengths, as shown below, screw a 1x facing strip onto the miter gauge to steady the work and have an assistant support the stock's dangling end.

2 For crosscutting identical lengths of material, clamp a length of scrap onto the *front end* of the rip fence, space the fence and block from the blade the length you want your pieces, and begin cutting. Or use a stop rod (see lower left sketch).

(continued)

SANDPAPER GLUED TO MITER GUAGE To prevent workpiece slippage

HOLD-DOWN CLAMP To keep workpiece in place while crosscutting and angle cutting

FACING STRIP ATTACHED TO MITER GUAGE For crosscutting or angle cutting long material

STOP ROD ATTACHMENT For crosscutting several pieces the same size

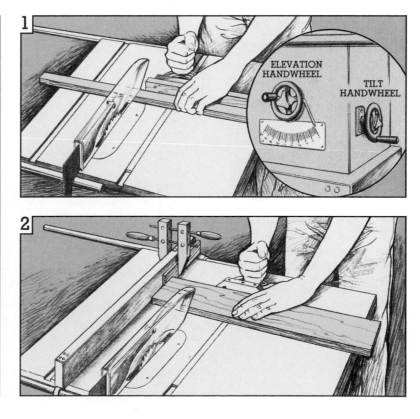

ELEVATION HANDWHEEL

TILT HANDWHEEL

Crosscutting *(continued)*

3 When cutting fairly wide cabinet components, such as doors or cabinet sides, begin by removing the rip fence from the saw table and locking the miter gauge at zero. Now reverse the miter gauge in the groove and place the workpiece firmly against it. Align the cut line with the blade and start the saw.

When you're halfway through the cut, stop the saw. Slide the miter gauge out of the back end of the groove and into the front and finish the cut as shown.

Rip Cutting

1 **With the saw unplugged,** adjust the rip fence at the necessary distance from the saw blade. To do this, use a measuring tape as shown to measure from the saw's *inside* teeth to the fence at both the front and back of the blade. This ensures having a parallel fence, which is important not only for accuracy but for safety, too. (If your blade needs adjusting, see sketch 1, page 67.)

Next, clamp featherboards (see pages 6-7) to the table and fence; these hold the workpiece snugly in place during the cut.

Now plug in the saw, flick on the switch, and begin sawing, slowly feeding the material into the blade. For long stock, have someone support the material as it comes off the saw table at the other end or construct a stand that will do the same thing. **To prevent your hands from getting dangerously close to the blade, use a push stick to finish the cut.**

2 In cases where you need to reduce material to less than 2 inches wide, **pull the plug** and remove the guard and antikickback apparatus. Then follow the ripping procedure shown in sketch 1. *(continued)*

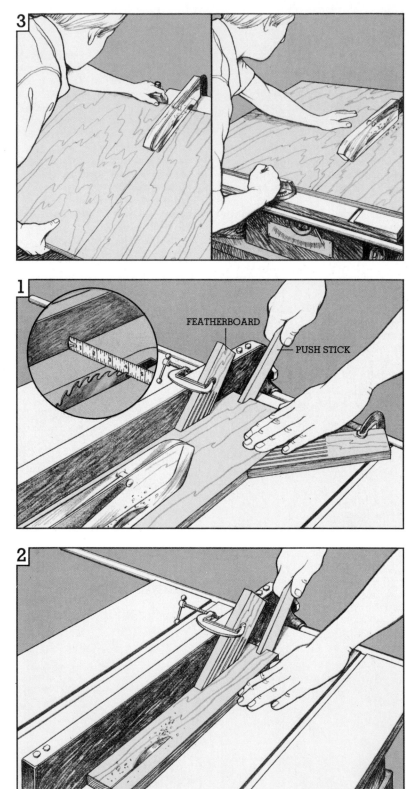

FEATHERBOARD

PUSH STICK

Rip Cutting *(continued)*

3 If rip cutting sheets of plywood, first **unplug the saw** and adjust the fence to the desired width (see detail in sketch 1). Then plug in the saw and have someone stand to one side to assist you in positioning the sheet on the table and against the fence as shown. (Don't put too much pressure on the fence, however; this could move it and result in a bad cut or cause the workpiece to bind.) Now, have your assistant flip on the switch underneath the sheet and begin sawing. **WARNING: If the blade binds during the cut, turn off the saw immediately.**

As you continue to feed the sheet, instruct your assistant to stand behind the saw to support that portion of the workpiece leaving the table.

Angle Cutting

1 Cut along the angled cut line scribed on the workpiece (see the detail in sketch 1), then adjust the miter gauge to the desired angle. (If you need to adjust the blade, see the copy that accompanies sketch 1, page 67.)

Now place the workpiece against the miter gauge, sliding it along until the cut line aligns with the blade. Remember to keep the kerf (the void created by a cutting saw blade) on the scrap end of the stock.

With the workpiece held firmly to the miter gauge, begin your cut.

2 For angle cutting large pieces of material, reverse the miter gauge in the channel and secure a facing strip to it. Adjust the gauge and align as shown in sketch 2, then plug in the saw and start sawing.

Once you've cut halfway through the material, turn the saw off and return the miter gauge to its normal place at the front of the table. Now complete the cut.

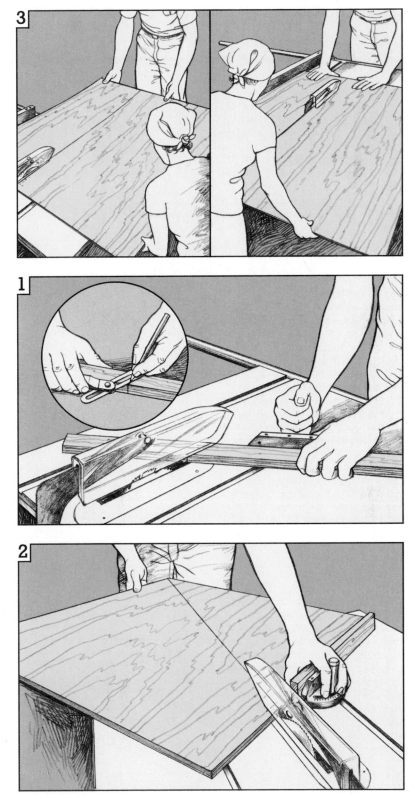

Beveling

1 After you know the degree of bevel you want, adjust a T-bevel accordingly. Then, hold this tool against the saw blade and table. Turn the tilt handwheel until the correct bevel angle is duplicated (see the detail in sketch 1, page 67). **NOTE: Before making any adjustment on the saw, pull the plug. Also, make sure the blade guard and spreader are tilted to match the angle of the blade.**

You may have to temporarily raise the blade to check for the proper blade angle and then later lower it to ⅛ inch above the thickness of the workpiece (see sketch 1, page 67).

2 If you're cutting across the grain, slip the miter gauge into the right-hand channel and lock the setting at zero. Placing the workpiece against the gauge, sight along the cut line until the blade and workpiece are in alignment. When you're satisfied, turn on the saw and ease the workpiece into the blade.

If making a bevel rip, as in the second example, position the rip fence with the stock held alongside it until the cut line agrees with the blade. Lock the fence in place and check to see if the front and back of the blade are equidistant from the fence. If they are, proceed as you would for any rip cut.

3 To bevel edges of a solid door for a raised panel look, start by fastening a wide, straight piece of 1 x stock to the full length of your rip fence. This prevents the workpiece from wobbling during the cut.

Next, draw the cut line, letting the width of the groove the panel is to fit into guide you in determining the width of the panel's edge (see detail in sketch 3). Allow a ⅛-inch difference between the raised and beveled portions of the panel. Now adjust the fence, remove the guard (since it interferes), clamp a featherboard to the table, and begin your cut.

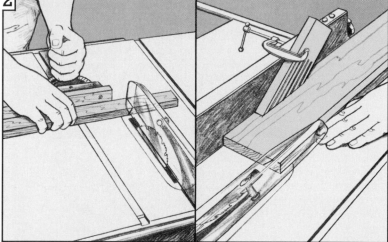

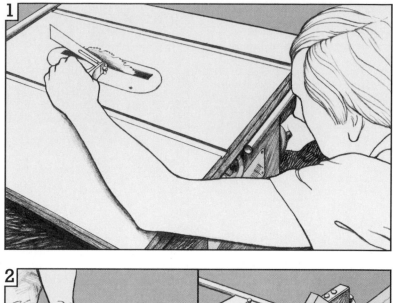

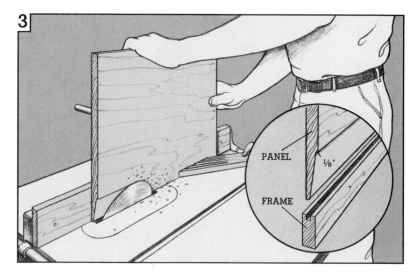

PANEL

FRAME

⅛"

Dadoing and Grooving

1 Prepare for the dado by **pulling the plug** and replacing whatever blade you have on the saw with a dado cutter of the proper width. (Refer to the instructions that came with the cutter for help with this.) Also, replace the regular table insert with the special dado insert. (Purchase this item when you purchase the dado blade.) Now adjust the dado cutter to the depth of cut marked on the workpiece.

If handling long stock, attach a facing strip to the miter gauge and have an assistant support the stock during the actual cutting.

Also, since the guard and spreader would only get in the way, remove them from the table.

As a final preparation, adjust the rip fence and accompanying scrap to serve as a stop, moving it to the right with each successive dado.

For a blind dado, clamp a stop block the appropriate distance along the other end of the fence as in the detail.

2 For cutting grooves, install and adjust the dado cutter as explained in step 1. Clamp on featherboards as needed, align the cut line on the leading edge and surface of the workpiece with the blade, and tighten the lock on the rip fence. Begin sawing.

For grooving along an edge, as with the door frame member shown at right, simply attach a featherboard to the table, adjust the dado cutter and fence, and begin cutting. **WARNING: Because this can be close-in work, use a push stick to keep hands away from the cutter.**

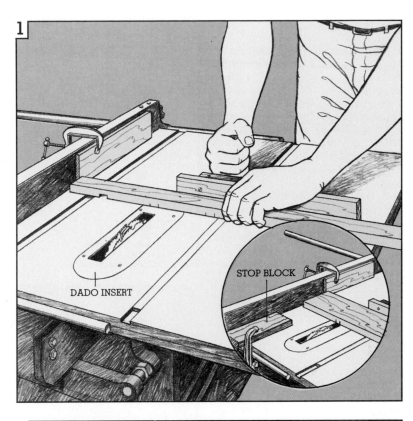

DADO INSERT

STOP BLOCK

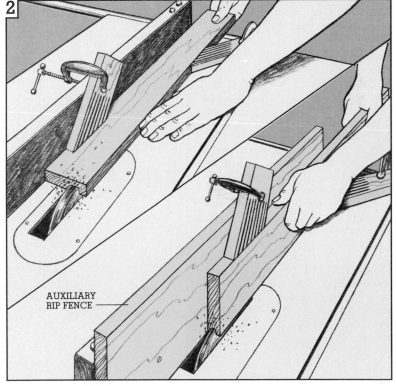

AUXILIARY RIP FENCE

Cutting Rabbets

1 If your project plans call for a rabbet, you'll be happy to know you don't need a dado cutter on your table saw to achieve the desired effect. As shown, a sharp combination blade will produce as good a rabbet as you'll want, though it requires you to make two cuts instead of one.

Prepare for the first cut by laying the workpiece flat on the saw table. Then, check the blade for square and adjust the depth. Now slide the rip fence (with attached wood scrap) over and adjust it so that the kerf is on the waste edge of the cut line. Clamp a featherboard as in sketch 1 and run the piece through.

Make the second cut by holding the workpiece vertically to the rip fence, making any blade depth and rip fence adjustments needed to align this cut line, and begin sawing.

If, on the other hand, you use a dado cutter, simply add the number of chippers needed to arrive at the correct rabbet width, **unplug the saw and insert and adjust the cutter,** and proceed with the cut.

2 If cutting a rabbet that's considerably wider than it is deep, as when with a half-lap joint, again, use a dado cutter. With the workpiece against the miter gauge, align its cut line with the cutter and slide the fence over. When the fence is flush to the workpiece end and parallel to the dado cutter, lock it in place.

Now plug in the saw and start sawing. Make as many passes as necessary to remove the waste material, shifting the workpiece farther away from the fence with each pass.

3 To rabbet a workpiece using a dado cutter (right), **unplug the saw** and slide the rip fence (with an auxiliary fence attached) the desired distance from the blade and lock it. With the blade on the scrap side of the cut line, adjust the cutter depth. Plug in the saw and start your cut.

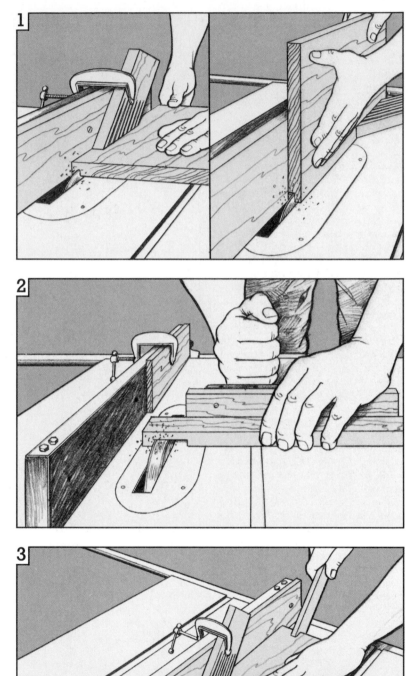

Router Work

Though you can use circular and table saws to dado and rabbet, be assured that the router performs these tasks best. Add to this the router's ability to fashion a fancy edge or decorate a surface, as well as trim laminate (see pages 58-59), and you'll agree there's no other tool quite like it. (Page 7 shows the router bits typically used in cabinetmaking and what each does.)

If you're a first-time user, acquaint yourself with the tool while practicing on scrap. You'll note immediately how the router jerks slightly in a counterclockwise direction when it first makes contact with the workpiece. This errant tendency doesn't have to be the rule, however, especially when there are so many guiding attachments available (several of which we show here). There are even inexpensive router tables available to which you mount the router underneath. Not only do these provide a smooth, flat work surface, but they also have adjustable fences for consistent, accurate cuts.

Keep in mind, though, that like other power tools, the router deserves your deepest respect. Aside from the safety and use tips on page 62, look over those in your owner's manual and below for the best possible results:
• **Wait until the bit reaches full speed before routing.**
• **Hold the router with both hands while operating it.**
• **Keep the router base flat on the work surface.**
• **For best control, use guides whenever possible.**

Dadoing, Grooving, And Edging

1 Once you've unplugged the router and secured the bit of your choice in the router's chuck, adjust

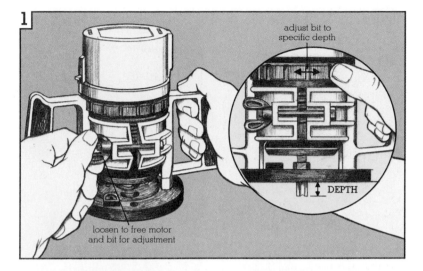

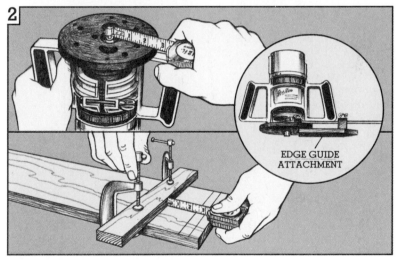

the bit depth. To do this, place the router on a flat surface and loosen the router base around the motor. On most models this involves turning a wing nut and adjusting the depth gauge—usually a calibrated ring or rotating drum—until the bit and subbase are even. (See sketch 1, above.) At this point, set the gauge at zero.

Now, position the router on the edge of a table and lower the bit to the desired depth. (Manufacturers advise making router bit adjustments and cuts in ⅛-inch increments.)

If your router doesn't have a depth gauge, place it on the edge of the workpiece and go by the

depth of the cut line. Now secure the base by tightening the wing nut.

2 Next, establish your straightedge location by taking a measurement from the edge of the bit to the outside edge of the subbase as shown above in sketch 2, part 2.

Mark on the workpiece where you want the outside edge of the cut. Then measure out from this line using the above measurement and clamp your straightedge here.

An alternative to this is to buy the versatile edge guide attachment (see detail, sketch 2) that rides along the workpiece edge during the cut.
(continued)

Dadoing, Grooving, and Edging *(continued)*

3 At right, we introduce you to related setup procedures that permit you to expand the uses of your tool.

To rout a blind dado, as shown in part 1 at right, clamp a straightedge the appropriate distance from the cut line. Then, clamp a stop block perpendicular to the straightedge the same distance beyond where you want the dado to end.

For grooving the edge of a narrow piece of stock, as shown in part 2, provide a flat, work surface for the router by sandwiching the stock between two lengths of 2x stock. Then attach a router guide attachment, adjusting it to the proper width.

When trimming inside or outside edges, as shown in part 3, simply use a bit with a pilot as your guide.

For best results, operate the router from left to right and counterclockwise around corners (see detail in sketch 3). If routing all four edges of a square or rectangular workpiece, reduce splintering by routing across the grain first, then with the grain.

Because of the bit size, depth of cut, and differences in workpiece hardness, expect the rate of travel to vary from cut to cut. **Don't force the tool or you'll slow the action of the bit and tear into the wood; on the other hand, go too slow and the high-speed bit could blemish the routed edges with burn marks.**

Adding Surface Designs

To route distinctive designs onto the face of cabinet doors with a router, start by tracing and cutting out a template of your design from plywood and clamp it to the workpiece. Allow room for the guide bushing (see detail A at right).

Then, with the router unplugged, attach the guide bushing. Adjust the bit to the desired depth, plug the tool in, and begin routing along the inside template edge.

Using an accessory as in detail B will help you achieve the same end result.

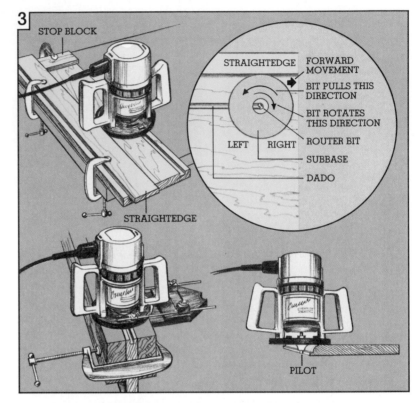

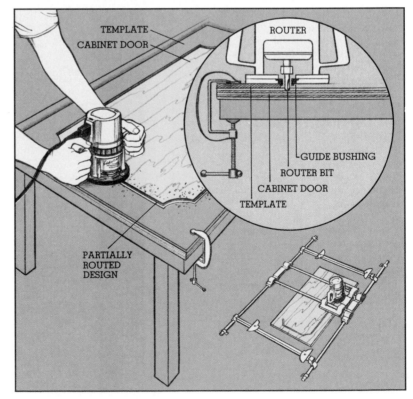

Joining Techniques

In the charts below, you'll learn about some of the more popular cabinetmaker's joints and how best to strengthen them. Also, on pages 75-77, you'll discover how to do the actual joining using nails, screws, or dowels and glue. Too, you'll learn what clamps to use.

To begin our discussion, however, look over these gluing and clamping guidelines:
• Always test-fit joining members prior to joining.
• When assembling a project, join each subassembly's members together first, then join the subassemblies, keeping all right-angle joints square.
• Whether assembling a carcass or attaching a face frame, use size 6d finish nails on corners; space them every 8 inches.
• Place a clamp at each glue joint end; for long joints, place a third clamp between ends.
• Follow glue container instructions for proper set time.

Choosing The Right Joint

Type of Joint	Description	Uses/Comments
Butt	Two or more members joined end to end, end to face or edge, or edge to edge.	Weak, yet good for carcass and face frame construction when pieces are glue joined.
Miter	Joint in which two members are cut at an angle, usually 45°, then fitted together.	Of medium strength. Preferred for molding trimwork on fine furniture cabinets.
Half Lap	A situation in which two members with recesses as wide as and half as deep as each is thick meet.	Strong. Excellent for face frames but requires considerable time and precision.
Dado	A joint formed when the end of one piece fits into the across-the-grain channel of another.	Strong and attractive. Used to support shelves in shelving units and cabinets.
Rabbet	Joint made when one member butts against another notched member. The notch is half the depth of the member it's cut into and as wide as the other member.	Strong. Commonly found in carcass construction, especially cabinet backs and drawers.

Joint Fortifiers

Corner Blocks	Dowels and Glue

Clamp Selector

Type of Clamp	Sizes	Uses/Comments
Handscrew	Jaw length from 4"-24"; jaw opening from 2"-17"	On finished surfaces where material is joined face to face and for securing workpieces and table saw helps. No protective scrap needed between jaws and workpiece, but jaws must be parallel to be effective. Expensive, but better quality than the C-clamp.
C-Clamp	Adjustable bolt opening from 2"-12"; throat depth from 2"-4½"	General purpose clamp that performs a variety of tasks including securing material face to face. Wood scraps needed between clamp and workpiece for protection. Relatively low in cost.
Pipe Clamp	Varies according to length of ½" or ¾" black pipe used, but ranges from 2-8'	Excellent for edge to edge clamping of boards and for holding together large members of a cabinet carcass or shelving unit. Similar to the bar clamp in looks and function, but less expensive.
Strap/Web Clamp	1" nylon belt 15' long	Good for clamping rounded and irregular shapes and for holding together carcass members. Moderately priced.
Miter Clamp	Holds members up to 3" wide	Ideal for clamping picture and cabinet face frame members at 90°. Openings permit installation of nails or screws. Inexpensive.

Joining with Nails and Glue or Screws and Glue

1 When joining with nails and glue, start by applying a bead of woodworker's glue evenly along the contact surface of one of the members.

For best results, use a brush or stick to spread the glue into a thin layer over the entire contact area. If dealing with end grain, which absorbs the glue, as in the plywood example at right, coat both of the joining members. Be sure to allow the glue to get tacky.

2 Fit the glued members together and secure them with clamps. (See the Clamp Selector Chart on page 75 for help with choosing the right clamps for the job.) If you're using pipe or C-clamps, slip in scrap wood between the clamp jaws and work to protect the work surface. After testing the joints for square, drill pilot holes and drive your nails.

To maintain snug corner joints, such as with face and door frame constructions, drill diagonal holes, then toenail members together as shown in sketch 2.

After driving your nails, go back and set them with a nail set. To ensure a strong glue bond throughout the contact area, remove the small scrap pieces between the clamp jaws and workpiece and insert a single long piece such as a 2x4 placed on edge.

3 When joining with screws and glue, first position and clamp the members together as you would when nailing. Then use a countersink/counterbore bit to drill the appropriate number of pilot holes. (Note in the detail at right how the desired finished look determines the depth of the holes.) Now, apply glue to one or both mating surfaces, allow it to get tacky, and drive the screws. Clamping here is optional.

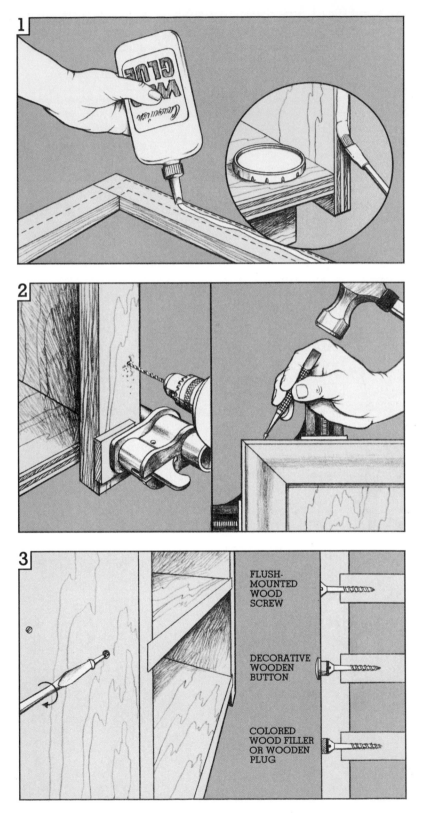

FLUSH-MOUNTED WOOD SCREW

DECORATIVE WOODEN BUTTON

COLORED WOOD FILLER OR WOODEN PLUG

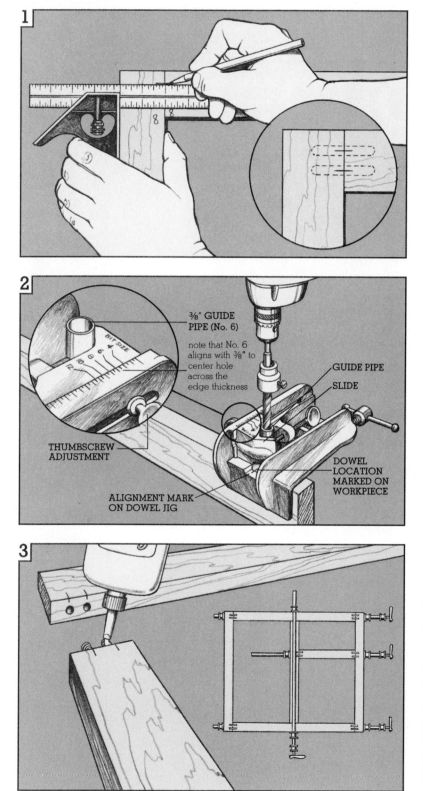

Joining with Dowels and Glue

1 First dry-fit the pieces using clamps. If you have a dowel jig like the one on page 7, place a combination square against the work at each joint location. Now strike two lines one-third of the way in from the appropriate frame edges to mark dowel locations, as shown.

To avoid a situation where the pieces refuse to fit together due to protruding dowels, plan your assembly so that the perimeter pieces are joined last. Also, it's a good idea to number the joining members of each joint in their order of assembly.

2 Select the dowel size you feel will do the job. Three ideally suited for face frames are $1/4$-, $5/16$-, and $3/8$-inch dowels. With any of these, you'll need to cut 2-inch lengths from dowel rods the right diameter, or buy a bag of dowels that have a spiral groove for holding more glue and beveled ends for easy joining.

Now, with the model dowel jig shown at left, secure the proper pipelike guide in the slide. Adjust the slide until the notch indicating your dowel's diameter on the slide aligns with the notch on the jig scale indicating one-half the thickness of the workpiece. This permits centering the dowel holes.

Next, locate the jig over one of the marks made on the workpiece and clamp it in place. Tighten the depth gauge on the drill bit allowing the bit to pass through the guide pipe and bore a 1-inch-deep hole. Now begin drilling. (Other brands of dowel jigs operate somewhat differently. If you have one of them, refer to their package instructions.)

3 Apply glue to the dowels and tap them into the holes. Assemble and clamp the members together, squaring all corners. After the glue begins to set up, go back and lightly scrape off any excess that oozed from between the joints. After waiting the prescribed time for the glue to cure, finish the job by sanding each joint smooth with a belt sander.

PROJECT POTPOURRI

Now that you're familiar with all the stages involved in constructing a cabinet or shelving unit, the time has come to put your newly acquired knowledge to work. Do this by either developing plans and constructing a project of your own design or by latching onto one of the attractive projects contained in this chapter.

If you choose one of the eight projects here, note that we've included complete step-by-step instructions for building each. For those steps that are particularly challenging, you'll find page references to other parts of the book where needed information is covered in more detail.

You'll also find overall project dimensions included with the projects, but don't let these lock you in as you draw up the details of your plans. Instead, feel free to alter the project's size to better suit the room where you intend to place the project. Or, you might choose to install another style of drawer or door than those shown. Should you make such a change, however, be sure to allow for it in your plans.

Crate-Style Shelving

Standing a full 73 inches tall, the handsome wood shelving unit shown here could do wonders for just about any bare wall in your house. While its sturdy shelves adjust to accommodate books, towels, or whatever else you wish to display, its light weight lets you move it from place to place without straining a muscle.

Add to this the ease and speed with which you can build the unit (see the steps below), and you'll agree that this is no ordinary crate.

1 Plan the dimensions of the project to suit your needs. (The unit shown here measures 32x14x73 inches.) For help with committing the plan to paper, see pages 34-35.

2 Cut the uprights and the shelf cleats to size, using ⁵⁄₄x2-inch stock.

3 Glue and nail the cleats to the up-rights, starting 1½ inches in from either end and spacing the cleats with the help of a 2-inch-wide spacer made from scrap.

4 Cut 1½x2-inch top spreaders and bottom members and secure them to the uprights with glue and nails. Square the corners as you go.

5 From ¾-inch plywood, cut the shelves and finish the edges with veneer tape (see page 41).

6 Fill all nail holes, then sand the unit smooth and finish it as desired (see pages 52-53).

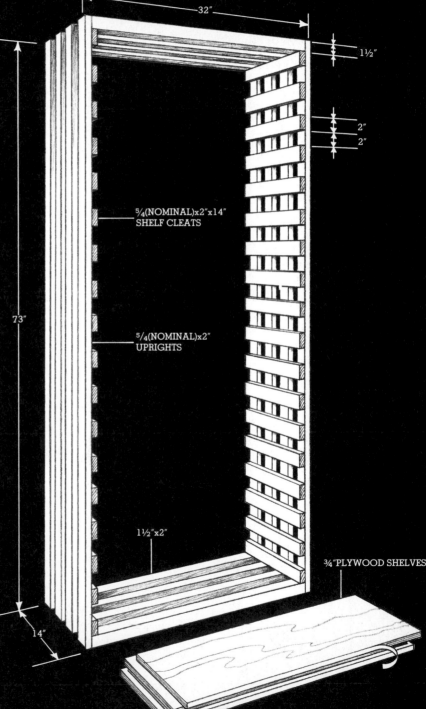

32″

1½″

2″

2″

⁵⁄₄(NOMINAL)x2″x14″
SHELF CLEATS

⁵⁄₄(NOMINAL)x2″
UPRIGHTS

73″

1½″x2″

14″

¾″PLYWOOD SHELVES

See-Through Room Divider

The rectangular opening above the counter, plus the two sets of sliding glass doors, allows this showy entertainment center to service both halves of the room it divides. The cabinet underneath, which opens on one side, provides ample storage for bar accessories, board games, or anything else you choose to keep there. But how hard is it to build this beauty? Just read over the steps below and find out. You're sure to be pleasantly surprised.

1 The project shown measures 60 inches across, 18 inches deep, and stands 66 inches high, but feel free to alter these measurements to suit your needs. With your plan on paper and materials purchased, cut all the pieces to size.

2 Cut grooves in the sides and cabinet divider to receive the shelf pilasters. While you're at it, cut rabbets and dadoes in the unit's sides and at the back edge of the top and bottom shelves of the lower cabinet, to accommodate the back (see pages 66 and 71-74).

3 Glue and nail the decorative panels to both sides, the top of the unit, and the bottom of the unit's upper storage cabinet. Make sure to center the panels, top to bottom and side to side.

4 Assemble the ¾x3-inch base members, square the corners, then center and secure the bottom shelf to the base.

5 Glue and nail the sides to the base and insert the remaining horizontal members in their respective dadoes and rabbets.

6 Install the center divider and back in the lower cabinet.

7 Fasten the pilasters in the center of the upper cabinet with L-brackets and screws. Install the glass door tracks as well, keeping them flush with the outside edges of the top and bottom.

8 Glue and nail ¾x1-inch face strips around the perimeter of the upper cabinet's opening in order to conceal the glass door tracks.

9 Hang the plywood doors on the lower cabinet. (For help, see pages 44-49.)

10 Fill all voids, sand smooth, and apply the desired finish (see pages 52-53). Install the glass doors in the tracks and the pulls to the lower cabinet doors.

11 Complete the project by screwing the remaining pilasters in the dadoes provided. Now install the shelf clips and the shelves.

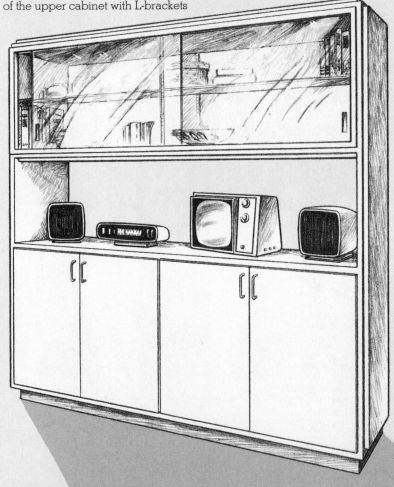

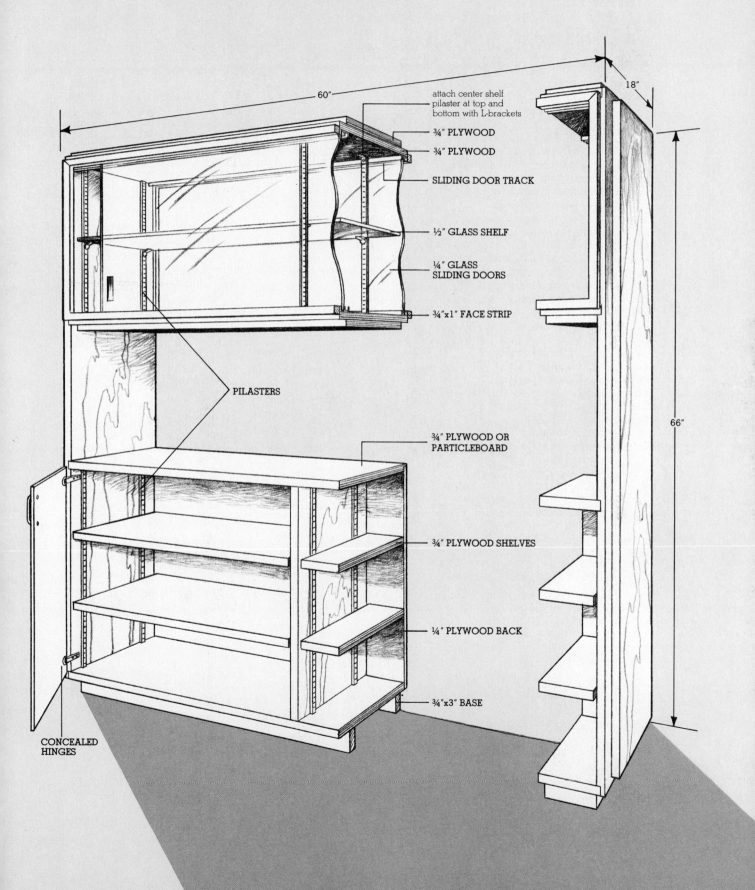

60"

18"

66"

attach center shelf pilaster at top and bottom with L-brackets

¾" PLYWOOD

¾" PLYWOOD

SLIDING DOOR TRACK

½" GLASS SHELF

¼" GLASS SLIDING DOORS

¾"x1" FACE STRIP

PILASTERS

¾" PLYWOOD OR PARTICLEBOARD

¾" PLYWOOD SHELVES

¼" PLYWOOD BACK

¾"x3" BASE

CONCEALED HINGES

Wall-Hung Storage/Study Unit

If you can build a basic box, then building this ingenious two-in-one project should cause you no trouble whatsoever. That's because the unit shown consists of nothing more than several boxes of varying size—some with doors, some without. Note, too, how one door folds down to make a nifty desk. If the arrangement or the number and size of boxes here doesn't quite jibe with your plans, rearrange these building blocks on paper (see pages 34-35 for help with finalizing your plan) until you find something that does suit your fancy. Then follow the construction steps below.

1 Cut all the individual box members, including backs, shelves, and doors to their exact plan dimensions. Don't forget to cut ⅜x⅞-inch rabbets at the back edge of the top and bottom and the sides of each box to accept the ⅛-inch back and ¾-inch ledger. Also cut ¾x⅜-inch rabbets at the top and bottom of the sides to accept the top and bottom. (If you need help with how to cut rabbets, see pages 66 and 72-74.) If you're using the plan as shown at right, use the measurements that have been indicated, keeping in mind the 6x6-foot overall dimensions.

After cutting the members, separate them into piles representing the different boxes to be built.

2 Assemble the sides, tops, and bottoms of the boxes using nails and glue. (For effective ways to join and clamp members, see pages 75-76.)

3 Install the backs, then the ledgers. Bevel these at 45 degrees, as illustrated in the detail.

4 Insert, center, and secure the shelves with nails and glue.

5 Screw the pivot hinges onto the doors (see page 46), and the piano hinge onto the fold-down desk leaf,

then mount the doors and leaf onto the appropriate boxes.

6 Decide where you want to hang the project. Also determine your stud locations. If you can't center the smaller boxes over two studs, either use hollow-wall anchors or toggle bolts to achieve the needed support from hollow walls. Now attach the matching 45-degree ledgers (one per box) onto the wall, beveled edge up.

7 Before fastening the remaining hardware onto the doors and desk leaf, fill all holes and paint or stain the project (see pages 52-53 for help with this). When the finish dries, place the boxes on the wall, working from the bottom up.

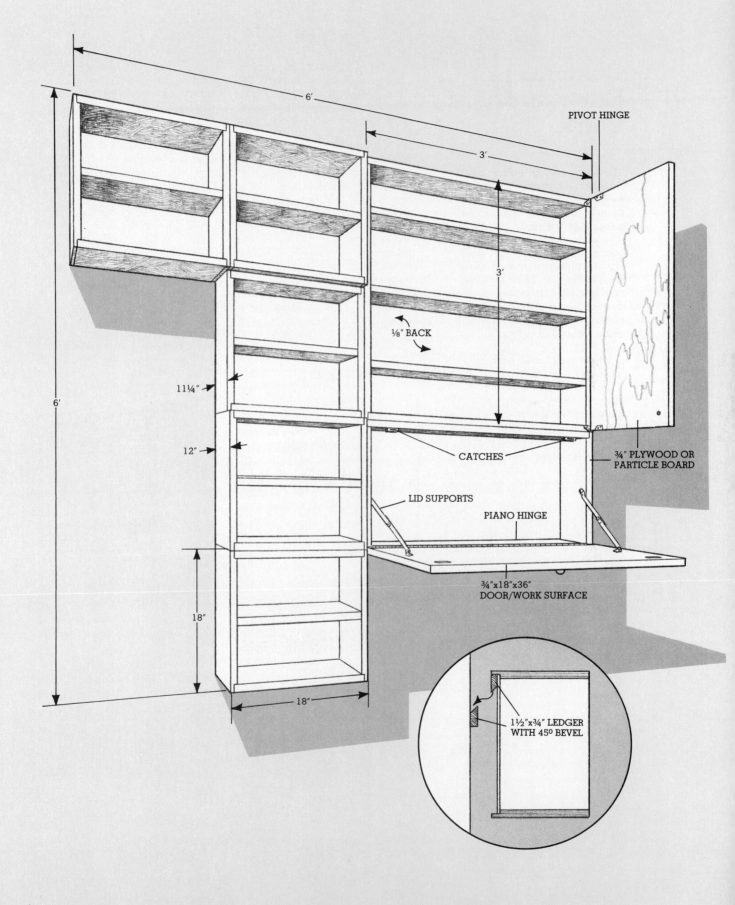

6'

6'

3'

3'

PIVOT HINGE

⅛" BACK

11¼"

12"

18"

18"

CATCHES

LID SUPPORTS

PIANO HINGE

¾" PLYWOOD OR
PARTICLE BOARD

¾"x18"x36"
DOOR/WORK SURFACE

1½"x¾" LEDGER
WITH 45° BEVEL

Custom Entertainment Center

The storage unit you provide for your electronic gear should have the following features: It should be strong enough to support the weight of a TV, stereo, and any additional components. It should be tailor-made to the items being stored. And, it must be attractive. The entertainment center pictured here meets all three criteria. To build it, follow the steps below.

1 Plan the dimensions of the entertainment center to satisfy your storage requirements. The unit shown, made from ¾-inch material, measures 66x67x16¾ inches. (For help with planning, see pages 34-35. For shelving span information, turn to page 25.)

2 Cut the uprights, top, and bottom to the same width. Then cut the shelves and dividers, making them ¼ inch narrower than the uprights. Cut all the pieces to the desired lengths.

3 Cut ¼ x ¼ -inch rabbets in the back edge of the sides, top, and bottom to receive the ¼ -inch back. Cut ⅜ x ¾ -inch rabbets at both ends of the uprights for the top and bottom.

4 Make ¾ x ¼ -inch dadoes on the upright and divider pieces at desired shelf locations.

5 Cut the back and the base members to the dimensions specified on the plans. (Here, the base is 1 inch shorter and ½ inch narrower than the cabinet.) Cut the base members 2 inches wide and to the correct lengths, miter their corners, and assemble the base with nails and glue.

6 Assemble the uprights, top, bottom, dividers, and back, again using nails and glue.

7 Attach the base to the cabinet.

8 Slip the shelves into the dadoes and against the back.

9 Cut ¾ x 1 ¼ -inch face frame members and install them either by the piece or as a completely constructed doweled face frame (see pages 75-77).

10 Fill all nail holes, sand, and finish with stain or other choice of finish (see pages 52-53).

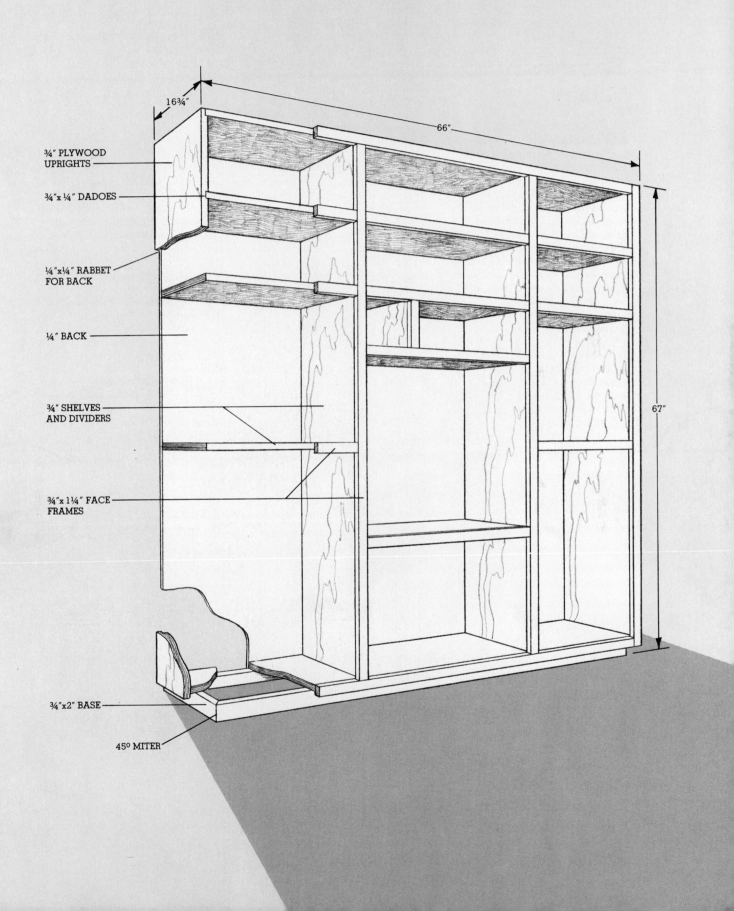

16¾"

66"

67"

¾" PLYWOOD
UPRIGHTS

¾"x ¼" DADOES

¼"x¼" RABBET
FOR BACK

¼" BACK

¾" SHELVES
AND DIVIDERS

¾"x 1¼" FACE
FRAMES

¾"x2" BASE

45º MITER

Sleek Bathroom Vanity

Add ample good looks to space-saving features in a bathroom vanity, and you have a combination that is hard to beat. The unit shown here offers all of this and more. Not only do its flush-mounted drawer and door fronts hint at an abundance of storage within, but its extended banjo counter top provides a refreshing change of pace from typical vanity installations. To build the unit, follow the steps described below.

1 Plan the dimensions of both the vanity and counter top to conform to your particular bathroom. This vanity unit shown here measures 21x36x30¾ inches; its counter top, including the 1-inch overhang at the end, spans 61 inches.

With laminate-covered projects such as this, when planning the sizes of flush doors and/or drawers, be sure to factor in the thickness of the laminate that you'll apply to the edges of the face frame and the doors/drawers. And because the curved edging work along the counter top is a departure from the standard construction of site-built counter tops, plan to cut the countertop sheet material so it overhangs the cabinet by ¼ inch. This, plus the ¾-inch face strip, will give you the proper overhang. (For information on typical vanity dimensions, see page 32. And for help with getting your project on paper, see pages 34-35.)

2 Cut the cabinet pieces according to the dimensions worked out on your plan. (See the cutting technique section beginning on page 68 for ways to cut and fashion your lumber.)

3 Assemble the cabinet as you would any base cabinet, following the instructions included on pages 37-51. Hold off installing the drawers and door until after you've laminated them (see step 5).

4 With a hole saw, cut holes in the cabinet back for your plumbing hookup. Then, install the cabinet as prescribed on page 54.

5 Cut the counter top to the required dimensions, using a saber saw to round corners where needed. Then cut a series of saw kerfs on the 1½-inch-wide face strip at those locations where you'll bend the strip around curved corners. Secure the face strip to the counter top using nails and glue.

6 Laminate the counter top and cabinet, including the door and drawers, following the instructions in steps 1 and 3-8 on pages 55-57.

7 Fasten the counter top support cleat to the wall by nailing it firmly to wall studs. If no studs are nearby, secure the cleat to the drywall using toggle bolts or hollow-wall anchors.

8 Install the counter top as described on page 57.

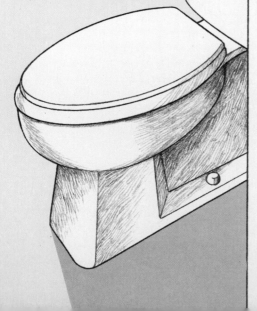

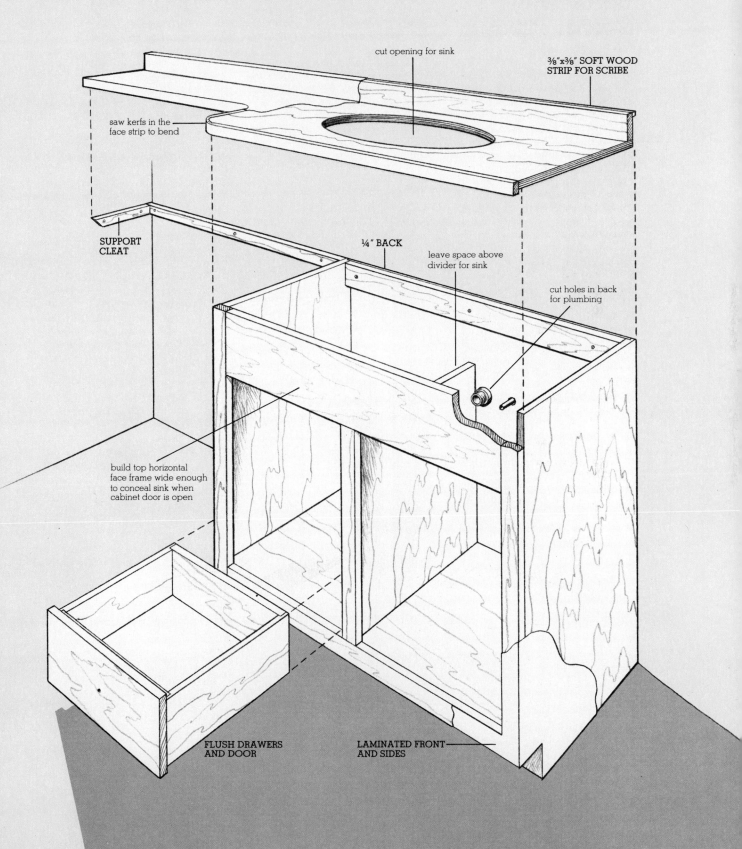

cut opening for sink

⅜"x⅜" SOFT WOOD
STRIP FOR SCRIBE

saw kerfs in the
face strip to bend

SUPPORT
CLEAT

¼" BACK

leave space above
divider for sink

cut holes in back
for plumbing

build top horizontal
face frame wide enough
to conceal sink when
cabinet door is open

FLUSH DRAWERS
AND DOOR

LAMINATED FRONT
AND SIDES

Hideaway Sewing Center

Who would believe that this handsome cabinet disguises a complete sewing center? Just open the wood-framed glass doors of the wall cabinet, swing out the base cabinet, and the center stands ready for plenty of sewing action.

Be sure to plan the unit's dimensions carefully (see pages 34-35 for help with this). The wall cabinet shown here measures 12x48x52 inches.

Base Cabinet

1 Out of ¾-inch plywood, cut out the sides and the 12-inch-wide foot board. From 1-inch (nominal) stock, cut a 4-inch-wide ledger, two 1-inch-wide foot board support cleats, and two 1½-inch-wide fake door attachment boards for the base cabinet.

2 Assemble the base cabinet members as shown in the sketch.

3 Cut and assemble the face frame members using dowels (see page 77), then attach the face frame to the base carcass.

4 Mitering the ends where needed, cut the base trim boards and attach them to the sides and front with screws and glue.

5 Cut out the base cabinet top from ¾-inch material and dowel 1¾-inch-wide strips to the top's side and front edges. Like the base trim boards, miter the ends of the strips where necessary.

6 Position the top on the cabinet so that you have a 1-inch overhang on the sides and front. Secure this by gluing and clamping.

7 Install a ¾-inch cove to the base cabinet, mitering ends where appropriate.

8 Build and install the flush-mounted fake doors, securing them with hinges and to the attachment boards (see page 44).

9 Using a saber saw, cut out an opening on the cabinet top for the sewing machine. Rout a recessed area around the opening the appropriate width and depth in order that the machine installs flush with the top (see pages 73-74 for information on routing).

Wall Cabinet

1 Out of ¾-inch material, cut out the sides, top, and shelves; from ¼-inch material, cut out the back; and from 1-inch (nominal) stock, cut two

2-inch-wide ledgers. The ledgers let you anchor the unit to the wall.

2 Dado across the sides for your shelves, and rabbet along the back edges of the sides and top to make room for the recessed back.

3 Attach the 1¾-inch strip to the top just as you did for the base cabinet top (see step 5).

4 Cut and assemble the face frame.

5 Assemble all the above-mentioned wall cabinet components using nails and glue.

6 Add the ¾-inch cove molding to the wall cabinet's overhang.

7 Build the door frames, rabbet the inside back edges of the frames to accept glass, then install the panes using screw-held buttons to keep them in place. Now attach the hinges and hang the doors onto the cabinet.

8 Hang the upper cabinet on the wall at the appropriate height (see page 54).

9 Fill all nail holes and voids on both cabinets, sand, and finish as desired.

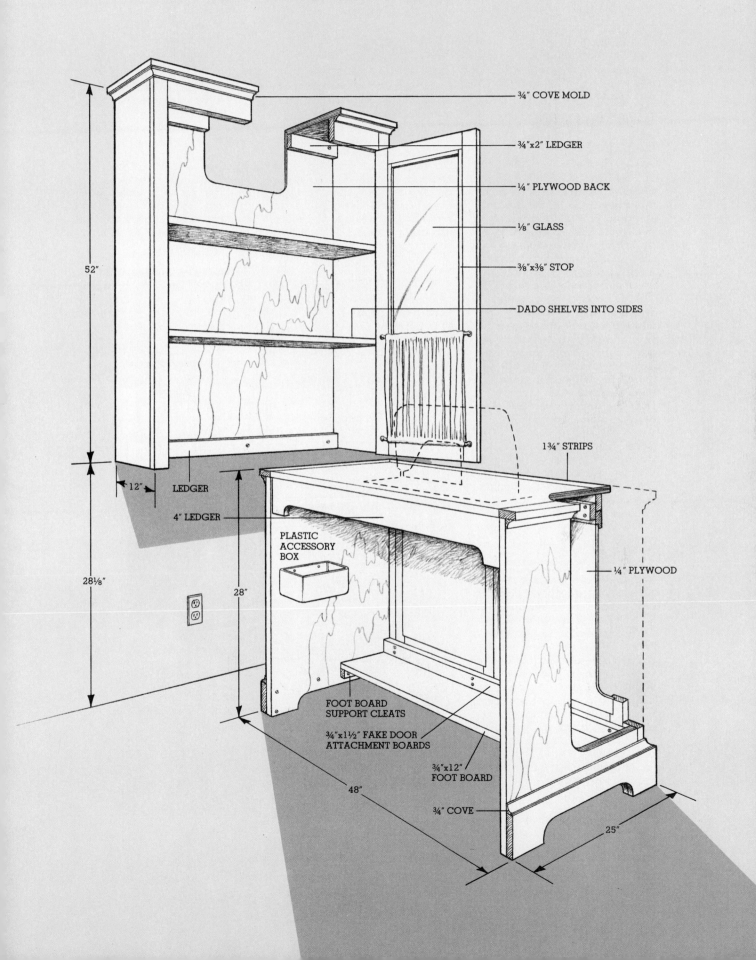

¾" COVE MOLD

¾"x2" LEDGER

¼" PLYWOOD BACK

⅛" GLASS

⅜"x⅜" STOP

DADO SHELVES INTO SIDES

52"

1¾" STRIPS

12"

LEDGER

4" LEDGER

PLASTIC
ACCESSORY
BOX

¼" PLYWOOD

28⅛"

28"

FOOT BOARD
SUPPORT CLEATS

¾"x1½" FAKE DOOR
ATTACHMENT BOARDS

¾"x12"
FOOT BOARD

48"

¾" COVE

25"

Stylish Computer Center

Because home computer retailers concentrate on selling only electronics, it is often left up to you to provide makeshift storage for your new purchase. The project shown on this and the following page may be just what you've had in mind. The unit has plenty of open and closed storage as well as enough counter space to accommodate your terminal and other supplies and paperwork. Also, depending on its placement, the center can serve as a room divider, with its upper shelving being accessible from both front and back.

1 Plan your project on paper, keeping in mind the dimensions of the computer terminal you wish to store. Should you want to build your project to the size of the one shown, note that it measures 38½x60x87 inches. (For help with planning, see pages 34-35.)

2 From ¾-inch material, construct the base cabinet and face frame as shown. When doing so, include the support and base ledgers as part of the carcass, but don't add the back. Also pay attention to the way the face frame has been cut and joined, as this offers the cleanest look.

3 Cut the counter top, banding edge strip, and ¾x3-inch backsplash, allowing room for the computer terminal's cable. Too, don't forget to notch the counter top to accommodate the wall-side shelving upright. Now laminate and install the counter top (see pages 55-57 for how to do this).

4 With the desk portion built (but not installed), cut out the shelving unit's sides. Dado across these where desired for shelves and rab-

bet along the top edge and partway up the back edge to allow for the ¾-inch top and ¼-inch back.

5 Cut the shelves, dividers, top, and back to size. Note that with the bottom shelf, a banding strip, backsplash, and two ¾x¾-inch cleats must be cut, joined, and laminated. (Again, see pages 55-57 for help.) This same shelf should, like the desk counter top, be slightly narrower than the shelving unit sides to accommodate electrical cords.

6 Treat all plywood edges that will be exposed to view in the finished product (see page 41).

7 Assemble the sides, top, shelves, and dividers. Glue and nail on the

¼-inch plywood back, then secure the shelving unit to the cabinet.

8 Fill all nail holes, and finish the cabinet as desired.

9 Move the unit into position against the wall, making sure it is plumb and level. Then support its open end by fastening the support ledger and wall-side shelving upright to wall studs using nails or screws.

10 Finally, build, finish, and install the drawers. See page 29 for how to construct overlay drawers, and pages 50-51 for how to install them.

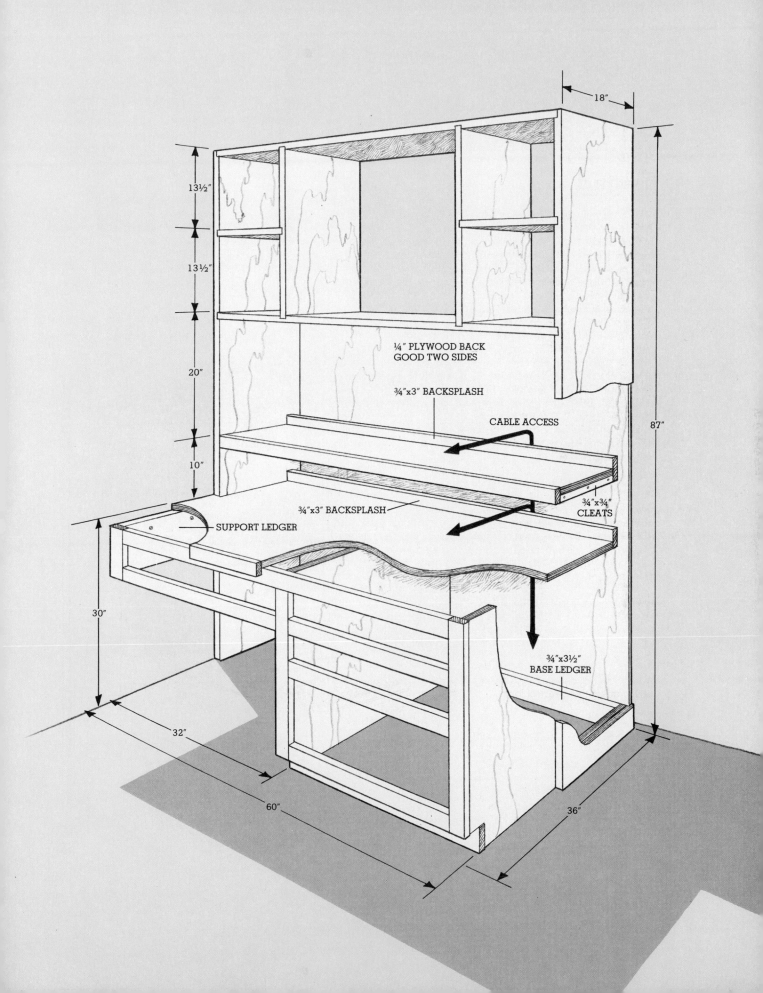

18″

13½″

13½″

20″

10″

¼″ PLYWOOD BACK
GOOD TWO SIDES

¾″x3″ BACKSPLASH

CABLE ACCESS

87″

¾″x¾″
CLEATS

¾″x3″ BACKSPLASH

SUPPORT LEDGER

¾″x3½″
BASE LEDGER

30″

32″

60″

36″

Space-Saving Kitchen Island

Adding an 84-inch-high kitchen island like the one shown here can quickly remedy most any storage problem your kitchen may have. With its roomy cabinet, you've got an ideal place to keep pots and pans; its spacious counter top provides a perfect work area for preparing food, serving, or any of a number of other kitchen activities. Note, too, the island's other storage features—including the overhead rack for hanging plants and the towel bars on the sides that let you show off your best kitchen linens.

1 Plan the project on paper to dimensions that will work well with your kitchen's size and layout. (For information on committing your plan to paper, see pages 34-35.) If you wish to build the project to the size shown here, it measures 24x42x84 inches.

2 After cutting out the 2x2 frame members, 1-inch blocking, and ¼-inch plywood panels for the sides, assemble the 2x2 frame members to form two rectangles.

3 Rout the 2x2 frames around the inside and outside edges to receive the inset ¼-inch plywood panels.

4 Using nails and glue, install the 1-inch blocking members, spacing them so the shelf cleats fasten to them. Now attach the ¼-inch inside panels to the frames.

5 Cut six 1¼ x¾-inch shelf support cleats, three stiles, the back, shelves, counter top, edge banding strips, and doors for the cabinet portion of the project. Make sure the length of the cleats allows for the ¼-inch back and face frame at the cabinet's front.

6 Screw the shelf support cleats to each of the uprights as shown.

7 After notching the center shelf to accept the middle stile, glue and nail the bottom and center shelves to the top edge of the cleats.

8 Fasten cabinet's end stiles to the cleats and shelving, and the center stile to just the shelving. Drive nails up through the bottom shelf into the center stile to secure it.

9 Glue and nail the back to the cleats and shelving.

10 Build, laminate, and install the counter top. (For help with laminating, see pages 55-57.) Remember to include the banding strips for both front and back.

11 Cut the members making up the upper ladder assembly from some 1-inch (nominal) stock. The longer members are 6-inch-wide lumber, the shorter ones, 5-inch lumber.) Now assemble the ladder and secure it to the unit's uprights with screws driven through predrilled holes in the blocking and into the ladder.

12 Glue and nail the remaining ¼-inch panels of the uprights.

13 Hang the cabinet doors (see pages 44-49).

14 Fill all holes and finish the cabinet with the desired paint or stain.

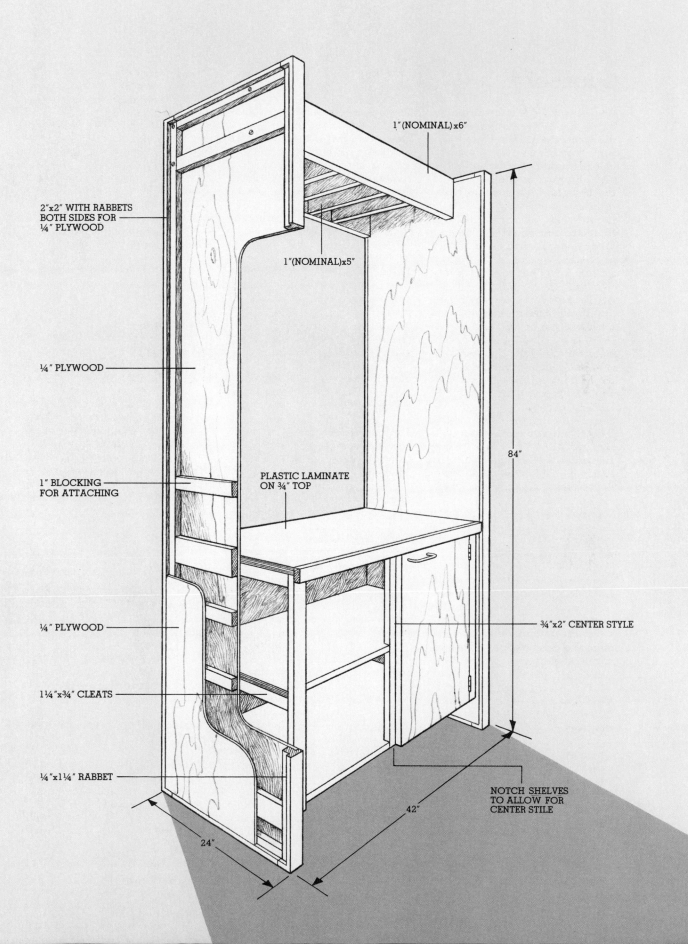

1″ (NOMINAL) x6″

2″x2″ WITH RABBETS BOTH SIDES FOR ¼″ PLYWOOD

1″ (NOMINAL) x5″

¼″ PLYWOOD

84″

1″ BLOCKING FOR ATTACHING

PLASTIC LAMINATE ON ¾″ TOP

¼″ PLYWOOD

¾″x2″ CENTER STYLE

1¼″x¾″ CLEATS

¼″x1¼″ RABBET

NOTCH SHELVES TO ALLOW FOR CENTER STILE

42″

24″

Glossary

Knowing a trade's terminology helps you better understand the trade itself. Below are some terms and definitions all cabinetmakers are familiar with. For any words used in the book and not covered here, refer to the index.

Abrasives—Materials such as sandpaper, pumice, and rottenstone used to smooth a workpiece for finishing.

Angle cut—A cut less than 90 degrees made through the width of a member.

Backsplash—Typically, a 3- to 4-inch-high length of material at the back edge of a counter top that extends its full length.

Bevel—An angle cut made through a workpiece thickness.

Blind dado—A channel cut across the grain that stops short of one or both edges of the workpiece.

Cabinet liner—An extra-thin and inexpensive laminate applied to the inside of cabinets for appearance and to prevent warpage.

Carcass—The framework of a cabinet to which shelves, a face frame, doors, and drawers are attached.

Contact cement—An adhesive spread on two surfaces that once dry bonds on contact when the surfaces are joined. (See *laminate*.)

Core material—The counter-top material to which a surface finish is applied.

Countersink—To drive the head of a nail or screw so its top is flush with or slightly below the surface of the surrounding wood.

Dado—A joint formed when the end or edge of one member fits into a channel of another.

Doweling jig—A metal device that clamps onto a workpiece edge or end and aids in accurately locating and drilling holes for dowels.

Drawer slides—The metal tracks or wooden cleats mounted to drawers and the inside of cabinets for suspending drawers and enabling them to open and close.

Face frame—The framework attached to carcass front. It may contain door and/or drawer openings.

False front—An inoperative drawer- or door-like panel used to simulate an operable drawer or door.

Grout—The material used to fill and seal ceramic tile joints.

Half-lap joint—A joint where both joining members are notched to half their thickness prior to joining.

Hollow wall anchor—A fastener, such as the toggle bolt and Molly™, that is used to secure objects to hollow walls.

Kerf—The void created by a saw blade as it cuts through a material.

Laminate—A hard, plastic decorative veneer applied to cabinets and shelves with *contact cement*.

Ledger—A horizontal strip (often wood) providing support for shelves and wall-hung cabinets and shelving units.

Millwork lumber—Any top-quality lumber (including molding) used in the building of shelving units, cabinets, and fine furniture.

Miter—The joint formed when two members that have been cut at the same angle (usually 45 degrees) meet.

Moldings—In cabinetmaking, specially milled strips of wood used as decorative trim for furniture-quality cabinets and shelving units.

Pilasters—Vertical shelf supports that can be mounted on or recessed into shelving or cabinet uprights.

Pilot hole—A small hole drilled into a wooden member to avoid splitting the wood when driving a screw or nail.

Rabbet—A joint formed when a notched edge of one member fits against the edge of another.

Rails—The horizontal members of a *face frame*.

Rip cut—To saw lumber or sheet goods parallel with grain pattern.

Scribe strip—A strip of filler wood (often ⅜"x⅜") attached flush with the top of back- and endsplashes to thicken their appearance and permit easy trimming.

Shim—A thin piece of wood or other material often used to fill a gap between two components to establish level or plumb.

Sliding door track—A set of grooves or runners along the front of a cabinet at top and bottom that hold sliding cabinet doors in place and permit them to slide.

Stiles—The vertical members of a *face frame*.

Tack cloth—A specially treated cloth used to pick up dust and other foreign particles from a smoothed surface prior to applying a finish.

Template—A pattern cut from wood, paper, or other material that serves as a guide for certain cutting tools.

Toekick—The notched space along the bottom of a base cabinet.

Veneer—A thin layer of decorative wood laminated to the surface of an inexpensive material such as particleboard or plywood.

Index

Page numbers in *italics* refer to illustrations or illustrated text.

A-C

Abrasives for wood, *16*
Adhesives and glues, 18
Angle cutting
  with circular saw, *64*
  with table saw, *69*
Backsplashes, laminated, *57*
Base cabinets
  carcass, *26*
    assembling, *37-38*
  for sewing center, *88-89*
Bathroom vanities, *86-87*
  scaled sketches, *34-35*
Beveling
  with circular saw, *65*
  with table saw, *70*
Butcher-block counter tops, 14
Butt-joint shelving, 41
Cabinets
  carcass, *26*
    assembling, *37-39*
  counter tops for. *See* Counter
    tops
  cutting list; cutting diagrams, *34-35*
  dimensions, *32-33*
  drawings, scaled, making, *34-35*
  face frames, attaching, *40*
  face-lift components, *17*
  finishing, *52-53*
  fronts
    false, attaching, *51*
    See also Doors; Drawers
  installing, *54*
  materials for. *See* Materials
  projects. *See* Projects
  shelves for, adding
    butt-joint, 41
    cleats, *41*
    edges, covering, *41*
    holes for clips/dowels, *43*
    pilasters, *42*
Carcass, cabinet, *26*
  assembling, *37-39*
Catches/pulls for doors, *21, 48*

Ceramic tile counter tops, 14, *60-61*
Circular saw, use of, 63
  angle cutting, *64*
  beveling, *65*
  crosscutting, *63*
  dadoing and grooving, *66*
  rabbeting, *66*
  rip cutting, *64*
  setting up, *63*
Clamps, 6
  selector chart, 75
Clear finishes for wood, *16*
  applying, *53*
Cleats, shelf, for cabinets, *41*
Computer center, *90-91*
Concealed hinges, *45, 47*
Corian® (high-density plastic)
  counter tops, 14, *59*
Counter tops, 14, *15, 55-61*
  marble, cultured and natural, 14, *59*
  plastic, high-density, 14, *59*
  plastic laminate, 14, *55-57*
    bathroom vanity, *86-87*
    post-formed, 14, *58*
  tile, ceramic, 14, *60-61*
  wood, laminated, 14
Crate-style shelving, *79*
Crosscutting
  with circular saw, *63*
  with table saw, *67-68*
Cutting
  router work, *73-74*
  safety tips, 62, 67, 73
  See also Circular saw, use of;
    Table saw, use of
Cutting list; cutting diagrams, 34-35

D-F

Dadoing
  with circular saw, *66*
  with router, *74*
  with table saw, *71*
Desks
  computer center, *90-91*
  fold-down, wall unit with, *82-83*
Divider, room, *80-81*
Doors, cabinet, *27*
  configurations, *31*
  designs, routing, *74*

flush, *28*
  hinges, *28, 30, 44-45, 47*
glass/plastic, *29*
  hinges, 30, *47-48*
hinges for. *See* Hinges
lipped, *27*
  offset hinges, *44*
overlay, *29*
  hinges, *29,* 30, *46-48*
pulls and catches, *21, 48*
sliding, *20, 30, 49*
style options, *31*
Dowel jigs; dowel work, *6,* 77
Drawers, cabinet, *27*
  configurations, *31*
  flush, *28*
  lipped, *27*
  overlay, *29*
  slides, *21, 50-51*
  style options, *31*
Edging with router, *74*
Entertainment centers, *84-85*
  room divider, *80-81*
Face frame, cabinet
  attaching, *40*
  flush door/drawer situations, *28*
False fronts for cabinets, *51*
Fasteners, 18, *19*
Fillers and sealers, wood, 16
  applying, *53*
Finishes for wood, *16*
  applying, *52-53*
Flush doors and drawers, *28*
  hinges, *28, 44-45*
    glass/plastic doors, *29-30, 47*
Frame and panel doors, *31*

G-M

Glass, kinds of, 12
Glass and plastic doors, *29*
  hinges, 30, *47-48*
Glues and adhesives, 18
Grooving
  with router, *74*
  with table saw, *71*
Hardware, 18, *19*
  drawer slides, *21,* 50
  lighting fixtures, *21*
  pulls and catches, *21, 48*
  See also Hinges
High-density plastic counter tops, 14, *59*

Hinges, *20*
  flush doors, *28, 44-45*
    glass and plastic, *29*-30, *47*
  glass/plastic doors, *29*-30,
    47-48
  lipped doors, *44*
  overlay doors, *29, 46-47*
    glass and plastic, *29*-30, *48*
Inset hinges, *44, 46*
Invisible hinges, *45*
Island, kitchen, *92-93*
Joining techniques, *75, 76-77*
Kitchen island, *92-93*
Laminated counter tops, 14
  installing, *55-58*
Lighting fixtures, cabinet, *21*
Lipped doors and drawers, *27*
  offset hinges, *44*
Lumber, millwork, 9-10
Marble counter tops, 14, *59*
Materials
  choice of, *23*
  counter-top. *See* Counter tops
  list, making, 35
  manufactured components, *17*
  millwork lumber, 9-10
  moldings, *11*
  sheet goods, 12
  wood-finishing, *16, 52-53*
  See also Hardware
Millwork lumber, 9-10
Moldings, *11*

N-R

Nails, 18
  joining with, *76*
Offset hinges, *44*
Overlay doors and drawers, *29*
  hinges, *29, 46-47*
    glass/plastic doors, *29*-30, *48*
Painted finishes for wood, *16*
  applying, *52*
Pilasters for cabinet shelves, *42*
Pivot hinges, *46*
Plastic, high-density, counter tops,
  14, *59*
Plastic laminate counter tops, 14
  installing, *55-58*

Plywood
  cabinets, *26*
  chart, 12
  rip cutting, *69*
Post-formed counter tops, 14, *58*
Projects, 78-93
  bathroom vanity, *86-87*
  computer center, *90-91*
  crate-style shelving, *79*
  entertainment center, *84-85*
  kitchen island, *92-93*
  room divider, *80-81*
  sewing center, *88-89*
  storage/study unit, *82-83*
Pulls/catches for doors, *21, 48*
Rabbeting
  with circular saw, *66*
  with table saw, *72*
Rip cutting
  with circular saw, *64*
  with table saw, *68-69*
Room divider, *80-81*
Router work, *73-74*

S-Z

Saws, 6
  use of. *See* Circular saw; Table
    saw
Screws, 18
  joining with, *76*
Sealers and fillers, wood, *16*
  applying, *53*
Self-closing hinges, 46
Sewing center, hideaway, *88-89*
Sheet goods, 12
Shelving
  categories, *24*
  fixed vs. adjustable, *25*
  materials for. *See* Materials
  needs, analyzing, 23
  projects. *See* Projects
  spans and spacing, 25
  supports, *19*
  See also Cabinets: shelves
Slab doors/drawers, *31*
Slides, drawer, *21, 50-51*
Sliding cabinet doors, 20, *30*
  adding, *49*
Staining of wood, *53*
Storage/study unit, wall-hung,
  82-83

Table saw, use of, 67
  aids for, *67*
  angle cutting, *69*
  beveling, *70*
  crosscutting, *67-68*
  dadoing and grooving, *71*
  rabbeting, *72*
  rip cutting, *68-69*
  setting up, *67*
Tile, ceramic, counter tops, 14,
  60-61
Tools, *6-7*
Vanities, bathroom, *86-87*
  scaled sketches, *34-35*
Veneer, wood, 12
Wall anchors, 18
Wall cabinets
  carcass, *26*
    assembling, *39*
  installing, *54*
  for sewing center, *88-89*
Wood-finishing materials, *16*
  applying, *52-53*